Remember

Eve

How The

Deceiver

Works In The

Believer's Life

Thaddeus & Erilynne Barnum

LONGWOOD COMMUNICATIONS

The Reverends Thaddeus and Erilynne Barnum
The Prince of Peace Episcopal Church
111 Cherryton Street
Aliquippa, PA 15001
(412) 375-5351

Published by:
Longwood Communications
397 Kingslake Drive
DeBary, Florida 32713
904-774-1991

Dedication

This book is dedicated to the children of the Mustard Seed Orphanage in Hoima, Uganda, East Africa, whose parents died of AIDS, and to the Rev. Canon John and Mrs. Harriet Rucyahana, who had the vision to make a Christian home for the lost babies.

The proceeds from this book are intended for the orphanage.

"All they asked was that we should continue to remember the poor, the very thing I was eager to do" (Gal. 2:10, NIV).

Acknowledgments

Remember Eve began on our sabbatical in Fairfax, Virginia, in the fall of 1982. A newspaper article told a story of parents who gave birth to a cross-eyed child. In their tradition, they believed cross-eyed children were mentally retarded. Embarrassed, they told family members the baby had died. The child grew up in the confines of a dark, wet basement. When the child was fourteen, a neighbor happened to see the eyes of the child peering out. Those sad eyes drove the neighbor to call the police. The boy was finally rescued after years of imprisonment. Upon examination, doctors found the child was not retarded. The parents had believed a lie. The story simply said the parents were deceived.

That story triggered our study of deception in the Scriptures. We soon found this theme dominated the apostolic message to the early churches. Most important to us was Paul's exhortation in 2 Corinthians 11:3 to remember Eve—the very thing we wanted to do in this book.

Erilynne and I went through numerous writings of this manuscript before it finally took shape. The last effort was the most time consuming. Erilynne and I want to thank our church family of the Prince of Peace Episcopal Church, Hopewell Township, Pennsylvania, who loved us, supported us, and prayed for us during the writing process. Special thanks to Joyce Wingett, who suffered through the many rewrites and the

Acknowledgments

many attempts to get our first book published. Thanks also to the Rev. and Mrs. Kenneth E. Ross, who encouraged us in our work and offered a wonderful critique to make the final text stronger and more accurate. For Murray Fisher, our publisher, and Mary Ellen Kammert, our editor, we give thanks to our Father in heaven. We pray the Lord Jesus Christ is glorified through this work and that it strengthens His church for the mission He has given to seek and save the lost.

Thaddeus and Erilynne Barnum
Easter Day 1995

Contents

Foreword

Remember Eve is an engagingly written book. It is clear, vivid and spritely paced. It addresses a much neglected but very serious problem in the Christian life: Spiritual Deception. Because of its content and also because of its style the book is both worthy of the reader's attention and a joy to read.

It is clear from the book that the authors have lived with this issue both biblically and pastorally. Their reflections are both exegetical and experiential. They let the light of Holy Scripture shine on the path of life as we all know it and have experienced it. The result of this is a book that opens our eyes to the reality of spiritual deception, to its nature and to its subtle manifestation, while at the same time offers the reader specific, practical guidance in addressing the issue.

As I read this book, I could only think of how little I had read on this subject over the years and of how little I had taught others about it. I suspect I am more the usual than the exception. Therefore we can thank our authors doubly for their dedication and hard work in writing this book. This is a greatly needed book and the ministry they have provided us is to be much appreciated. We all need the awareness and wisdom found in these pages, particularly those people who are in lay or ordained pastoral ministry in the Christian Church.

I commend this book to you with great enthusiasm. Read carefully, read well, and apply it.

John H. Rodgers, Jr.
Professor for Systematic Theology, Trinity Episcopal
    School for Ministry
Dean/President Emeritus
Rector, St. Stephen's Episcopal Church, Sewickley,
    Pennsylvania

DECEPTION DEFINED

Deception is like the king in the fairy tale who walked out his palace doors and rode through the streets of town, publicly parading with no clothes on. Why? Because he believed—he really, honestly, sincerely believed—he was wearing royal garments.

It's like the child at the school cafeteria who smelled his ice cream because his best friend told him it smelled funny. He believed his friend told the truth—up to the moment the ice cream smashed into his face. It's like the amateur art collector paying thousands of dollars simply because the salesman dazzled him with the line, "This is an authentic Picasso, the only signed Picasso on the market in the entire world! It's the opportunity of a lifetime!"

Prologue

Deception gripped Sammy, who never boozed during the week. But come Friday, he binged. Although friends and family urged him to get help, Sammy believed he was in control of his liquor. He didn't know he was caught in an addictive world that's based on a deceptive lie: "I'm not an alcoholic, I'm in control of my life and my drinking. You think I'm like those drunkards on the street? Not old Sammy!"

Jane was deceived even as she lay in the hospital bed with multiple wounds to her face and body. Love had blinded her. Her friends had warned, "Tom's a violent man. He's abusive. Stay away from him or you're going to get hurt!" But Jane thought differently. She saw a diamond in the rough, someone who would change with a little tender loving care. She honestly believed Tom loved her and wouldn't hurt the one person who truly loved him.

Does this sound familiar? Didn't we grow up in a world that warned us about deception? How often I remember my parents and grade school teachers telling me, "Never talk to strangers!" Why? Because they know there are people who steal children. How does it happen?

I'm walking home from school alone. A stranger meets me on the road and calls me by name. He says, "Thad, your mommy's running errands. She told me to pick you up from school today and play with you at home until she gets there. Come on, hop in my car!" He holds out his hand as a sign of friendship. He offers me candy. My mouth waters. The story sounds good, feels right. He seems like a nice man. He knows my name—so how could he be a stranger? I accept his invitation.

And that's that.

Deception is a hell-struck blinding that tricks the eyes into seeing what's not really there. The mind is twisted into believing a lie, bewitched like the thirsty desert wanderer who sees through the wall of heat to an oasis. The oasis cries out,

9

seductively inviting him to come drink. And when he follows the empty vision, yearning to taste from the cool desert springs, he finds a waterless, black-hole mirage that disappears.

It is a distorted, cruel world. The innocent are always the victims, ever too quick to trust their environment; always believing, always hoping, always seeing the world as innately good, without the potential of evil. The naive do not detect the malicious counterfeits in our society. They are like graceful fawns springing through the forest, wholly unaware that one taste of the bait releases the trapper's snare.

"Beware," I was told by my parents and teachers, because the unthinkable could happen to me. And I did heed the warning, for the fear of being abducted and never seeing my family again was real, and it scared me. Only later did I realize that it was a healthy, protective fear. Yes, it broke my innocence.

But that fear taught me to beware of the schemes of strangers, and because of it I took the necessary precautions. I never walked home alone. I watched and listened for strangers who wanted to engage in conversation. I remembered the warning.

The danger of being deceived looms for anyone who thinks, "It could never happen to me!" These cannot hear the warning. They skip through life fearlessly, not knowing the cunning power of the devil dressed as a friend. They are unaware of the danger and therefore are easy targets for the deceiver.

And then it happens. The trapper's snare triggers; the king realizes he's naked; the ice cream drips from the child's face; the alcoholic hits bottom; the woman blinded by love is abused; the stranger drives away with the child. It's that moment of dark terror: *You suddenly know!* You've been mercilessly tricked— thrown into hell's flame—just like that, with no way out.

That is deception.

The Deceiver Within the Church

The Bible teaches us that Satan "deceives the whole world" (Rev. 12:9). Over the years, many Christian books have been written for the purpose of identifying the world's thinking. Too often, secular doctrines have crept into the teaching of the church. Today, a number of Christian ministries are devoted to exposing worldly deceptions (such as the rise of secular humanism or the current rage for dime-store psychology that promises complete self-fulfillment) and their impact on believers. The authors rightly warn the church not to be conformed to worldly philosophies which, when spoken from the pulpit, appear godly.

Another area of great concern is religious deception. By definition, this includes any religious group that is set apart from and out of active dialogue with the Christian faith handed down to the present-day church. Again, our bookstores are chock-full of material alerting the believers, especially when the religious group is Christian-like, Bible-based and using the name of the Lord Jesus Christ (such as the Jehovah Witnesses, Mormons, Christian Science, Scientology, including the various cults and occult which have recently arisen with the generic term "New Age" — to name a few.) The warning against religious deception has been rightly sounded in our day.

What seems to be lacking is a book written on the course of deception within the community of believers. Although Satan deceives the world and fathers religious imitations, we must remember: Deception did not originate in the world! It started in the glory of Eden, the garden where God and man walked together.

The deceiver has not stopped this work. He remains active in churches today.

The New Testament invites us to wrestle with this issue and to do it with utter seriousness. On more than one occasion Jesus took His disciples aside and warned them, saying, "Take heed that no man deceive you" (Matt. 24:4, KJV). He wanted them to know an ancient truth: the deceiver targets those who belong to the Lord.

Paul did the same thing with his disciples. Before leaving Ephesus for the last time, he instructed the elders to be awake, on the alert! He plainly stated that deceivers would arise within the church "to draw away the disciples after them" (Acts 20:30).

John's first epistle was written "concerning those who are trying to deceive you" (1 John 2:26). Peter warned his readers that "there will also be false teachers among you, who will secretly introduce destructive heresies" (2 Pet. 2:1). Jude wrote that deceivers had already crept into the church unnoticed (see Jude 4).

The attack is in-house, it is done secretly, and its aim is to draw the disciples away. The New Testament warning rings loud and clear. All the apostles knew the great danger and their fundamental responsibility to issue the warning in their epistles and in their preaching. Oh yes, it is an ancient truth: The deceiver targets the faithful. His work, done within the church, is the subject of this book.

It Began in the Garden

It's Paul who paves the way back to Eden.

The church at Corinth looked alive in Christ. But, in truth, the deceiver had come and, as always, he was dressed in disguise. This time it was the dangerous costume of an apostle—a false apostle—even called an "angel of light," who preached in their pulpit (2 Cor. 11:14). He seemed to be sent from God. And the Corinthians believed.

But not Paul. He knew how deception worked. He knew how the serpent tricked Eve in Paradise and that Satan was still at work deceiving the churches in like manner. Therefore, Paul wrote the Corinthians insisting they also know how deception works.

He took us back to the garden. He made us remember Eve:

12

> For I am jealous for you with a godly jealousy; for I
> betrothed you to one husband, that to Christ I might
> present you as a pure virgin. But I am afraid, lest as
> the serpent deceived Eve by his craftiness, your
> minds should be led astray from the simplicity and
> purity of devotion to Christ (2 Cor. 11:2-3).

The comparison is plain and simple: Just as the serpent deceived Eve by his craftiness, so that same serpent was at work in the Corinthian church. His mission: to draw the church away from her devotion to Christ.

Paul was afraid for them. He went back to Eden and caused the Corinthians to recall the first deception. He put a holy, righteous, godly fear into the hearts of all who could hear him. That apostolic voice, like the sound of my parents and teachers, cried out the warning: *Beware of the original stranger!*

And that voice still cries out. Paul knew the truth of Genesis 3.

Paul said this about Old Testament Scripture: "For whatever was written in earlier times was written for our instruction, that through perseverance and the encouragement of the Scriptures we might have hope" (Rom. 15:4). In this case Paul used Genesis 3 to instruct the Corinthians. In the midst of their own situation, he reminded them of the garden—and the Eden deception.

If we're going to understand how deception works within the church and within our own lives, we must follow Paul's example and return to that same garden, back to Genesis 3. We must ask the questions: What did happen between Eve and the serpent? How was she deceived? Could it have been prevented? For by hearing the instruction of Scripture, we will gain perseverance and encouragement. We will know how to prevent deception in our churches. We will know how to stop the serpent of old.

Blinded

All my defenses rise with a subject of this nature. Somehow I feel comfortable pointing my finger at the world and crying, "How deceived you are!" or saying to certain religious groups the words of my Savior, "You serpents, you brood of vipers, how shall you escape the sentence of hell?" (Matt. 23:33). It's okay as long as no one is pointing at me.

But when I look into the mirror of my own soul, the resistance goes up: What, me deceived? No way!

Pride screams inside, "But I know the Lord Jesus! I've been a Christian since I was a teenager. I've been preaching the Scriptures since I was twenty-two. I hold a master's degree, and I pastor a church by profession. Don't these credentials protect me? How can I be deceived? Plus, isn't deception for the naive, the young in faith, the uneducated?"

I was blinded—until I heard the sound of apostolic warning: As it happened to Eve in the sinless beauty of Paradise, so it could happen to me today. That truth burned godly fear deep into my heart.

I saw it in the eyes of a churchgoer—someone who professed Jesus as Lord. He sat in my office, defending his God-given right to divorce his wife of twenty years. "Things aren't the same anymore. We don't love each other. Plus, the Lord has given me a new woman to love!" He believed he was right, square in the middle of God's perfect will. No amount of discussion could persuade him. He was blinded.

Another man, a leader in the church, asked me to stand with him on the doctrinal issue of abortion. He was obsessed by it. Even though his doctrine was correct, he was a man filled with deep-seated anger. He began to put his agenda forth in our church. His militant style caused a schism within three months' time. There were those ready to join this man's cause. They were caught up in his bitter enthusiasm. But others backed away. They believed in his doctrine but not in his method. Two groups formed. Both justified their positions biblically. The command to love one another disappeared altogether. Our eyes were on that man and his agenda—and away from our Father in heaven. There was division in the church—the sure sign of Satan the deceiver.

I suddenly found myself surrounded with believers caught in deception. I heard an endless stream of words—the confident assertions coated in God-talk: "I'm doing what the Lord wants me to do. Praise God! It feels right." They sounded like the man who said to me, "It feels right to divorce my wife. The Lord has led me every step of the way!" I saw naked kings, unsuspecting fawns, desert travelers. I saw the Eden stranger at work in my generation.

I wanted to ask, "Why are they so blind?" But I remembered the words of my Savior: "And why do you look at the speck that is in your brother's eye, but do not notice the log that is in your own eye?" (Matt. 7:3). That mirrored back to my own soul.

The proverb is true: "The fear of the Lord is the beginning of wisdom" (Prov. 9:10). Fact: deception is still at work. The warning of the New Testament belongs to me and to my house first. Yes, the deceiver wants to lead me away from the simplicity and purity of devotion to Christ. To know that is to know a healthy fear of the Lord. So I stand on the alert for the stranger, as I did as a boy. But I know that warning does not stop with me.

The Scriptures proclaim this message as part of our apostolic witness of the gospel. The warning belongs, with passion and fear, at the very heart of the church. For the statement is true: As the serpent came to Eve, as he came to the Corinthians, so the same deceiver comes to the churches of Jesus Christ today.

The warning must sound again, lest the stranger comes and we're caught off guard, like Eve.

It's time to put godly fear into our hearts.

For this reason, *Remember Eve* makes its way back to the beginning, back to the story of a serpent who, in the cool of the day, happened to strike up a conversation with the woman of God.

Genesis 3 will become our home. We'll take front row seats as the serpent makes his attack. Second, we will discover why Eve felt an attraction to the tree of disobedience and how she ate—truly believing it was God's will. Third, we'll know the barrenness of Eve's anguish after deception had been accomplished. The last section, the awakening, deals with this question: How can we spot and stop deception in our churches today?

But we must go back to Eden—and remember Eve. Why? Because it could happen to us.

Part I

THE ATTACK

One

THE SERPENT OF OLD

S tudying Genesis 3 is often a new experience for believers. Many people bypass the first ten chapters of Genesis. The debate between creation or evolution, faith or science, literal truth or myth, often clouds our ability to read these Scriptures.

We ask, "Did God create the world in seven days? Did He start with two people? Are we sure Methuselah lived 969 years? What about the flood story? Do we actually think a real serpent met Eve by the knowledge tree, in a real place called Eden?"

For some, it's easier to start with the story of Abraham.

I don't doubt the importance of these questions. But Paul hurdled them in a single bound when he warned the Corinthians to remember how "the serpent deceived Eve" (2 Cor. 11:3). Without question, Paul believed in the scriptural account of Eden. So do we. But if this issue troubles you, step beyond it for now. Hear Paul's words to the church at Corinth: "Whether you believe Genesis 3 is historically accurate or not, it's happening in your midst—now! That serpent has come to you!" With this perspective, Genesis 3 could never be considered a myth at all. At the very least, it is a real story about our lives right now.

And so we turn to Genesis 3 to draw from the deep well of truth found in this passage from God's Word. I urge the reader to enter through the portals of Eden without hesitation, into the conversation between the serpent and the woman, and to learn with expectation the course of deception from the beginning of time.

The Serpent

Our introduction to the Eden serpent is startling: "Now the serpent was more crafty than any beast of the field which the Lord God had made. And he said ..." (Gen. 3:1). Let's make it clear: This serpent was different than any creature on earth today.

First, *the beast spoke!* He had the ability to communicate in Eve's language. Eve gracefully responded, suggesting that talking serpents were a common experience in her Paradise home.

Second, *the beast walked!* When God later cursed the serpent, He said, "On your belly shall you go" (Gen. 3:14). Well, what does that mean? Clearly the assumption can be made that, before the curse, garden serpents walked in an upright position. Then, after the curse, the serpent race was condemned by God to travel on its belly.

Third, *the beast was beautiful!* This is hard for us to believe—a beautiful serpent! But there is much to learn from Eve's calm reaction to the serpent. It is important to remember that Eve was brought forth from Adam's side into a perfect world, in the image of the perfect God. Obviously, if the serpent had appeared in anything less than perfect form, Eve would have known it instantly—and it would have undoubtedly repulsed her. It would have been her first contact with evil. It is remarkable that she was not repulsed.

The serpent was Eden-perfect.

In the cool of the day, like any other day in God's garden, Eve had a conversation with one of the creatures. This time it was a serpent. Although it was "crafty," it was still a normal serpent—a talking, walking, beautiful creature of God. To Eve this one looked like all the others "which the Lord God had made." There was nothing in his presentation to make her think otherwise.

But here we must exercise caution. It is easy for students of the Bible to identify the serpent as Satan. In Revelation 12:9 we read, "And the great dragon was thrown down, the serpent of old who is called the devil and Satan, who deceives the whole world." Here we see the unquestionable truth; the serpent of old—the one Eve encountered in Eden—is none other than the devil and Satan.

But let's make an important point: Satan didn't come as himself—the newly fallen angel of darkness. He came as a talking, walking, beautiful serpent, dressed in the appearance of one of God's perfect creatures—incognito. The prince of outer darkness had disguised himself in the beauty of Paradise light.

We must rightly understand his position: Satan was inside the God-made serpent costume.

It is the first of deception's ways: deceivers come in disguise, dressed for the party. "And no wonder," Paul writes, "for even Satan disguises himself as an angel of light" (2 Cor. 11:14). It is a gruesome truth. But since the very beginning, the devil has possessed the ability to wear the garments of God's kingdom. Of course, it's all a trick. But it's a trick that works.

In Paradise we meet Satan dressed as a serpent-in-light.

The New Testament Wolf-Sheep

Jesus gave us the warning. In Matthew 7:15 He said to His disciples: "Beware of the false prophets, who come to you in sheep's clothing, but inwardly are ravenous wolves."

In these words Jesus used traditional biblical imagery. In God's eyes, His people are like sheep. As Psalm 100:3 says (using but one example), "We are His people and the sheep of His pasture." Of course, the wolf is the picture of the sheep's enemy.

Jesus was most definite: The "ravenous wolves," who desire nothing more than to forcefully capture and consume sheep, will "come to you." But they won't look like wolves. They will come "in sheep's clothing." Dressed looking like us. Sheep on the outside; wolves on the inside. No wonder our Savior said to beware.

They look Christian, act Christian, and speak "Christianese." They look like sheep, smell like sheep, "bah-bah-bah" like sheep and do "sheepy" things like we do sheepy things!

They are not sheep but ravenous wolves, not true prophets but false prophets.

To the spiritually untrained eye and to all the natural senses, there is no way to distinguish sheep from wolf-sheep. If you're not on the alert, you will never detect the deceiver crouching inside the church fellowship waiting to pounce. Just as Jesus taught us:

> Not everyone who says to Me, "Lord, Lord," will enter the kingdom of heaven; but he who does the will of My Father who is in heaven. Many will say to Me on that day, "Lord, Lord, did we not prophesy in Your name, and in Your name cast out demons, and in Your name perform many miracles?" And then I will declare to them, "I never knew you; *depart from me, you who practice lawlessness*" (Matt. 7:21-23, italics added).

21

The watchman's voice shrieks through the night. It is the battle cry. The enemy is on the approach, ready for war. Oh, the bitter sound of His alarm! Hear His voice: *The enemy is inside the camp.*

But how shall we recognize the enemy? They call out, "Lord! Lord!" and then prophesy the word of the Lord—in Jesus' name. They stand in our midst and ward off the devil by casting out demons right before our eyes. Worse yet, these ravenous wolves are able to perform signs and wonders—mighty miracles of power.

These abilities seem to validate (not deny) their Christian faith. Won't the church welcome them as chosen instruments of the Lord Jesus? Won't we stand in awe of their God-given gifts, maybe even make them elders, ministers over thousands, mentors of the young?

How will we know sheep from wolf-sheep? For the Lord Jesus Christ, the shepherd of the sheep, makes a clear distinction. He will turn to those deceivers "on that day" and say, "I never knew you; depart from Me, you who practice lawlessness."

The deceiver is an exact look-alike. He is a counterfeit that looks all too real.

These words from Scripture inform us that the matter of deception is dangerous to the well-being of the church. It forces us to perceive our world in a new way: The enemy does not always come from the outside looking like Satan and his hosts. He comes on the inside, looking like us. Jesus' command, "Beware," takes on a new meaning when we understand the nature of wolf-sheep.

Paul proclaimed the same danger to the Ephesian elders:

> Be on guard for yourselves and for all the flock, among which the Holy Spirit has made you overseers, to shepherd the church of God which He purchased with His own blood. I know that after my

departure savage wolves will come in among you, not sparing the flock; and from among your own selves men will arise, speaking perverse things, to draw away the disciples after them. Therefore be on the alert (Acts 20:28-31a).

Paul addressed the elders, the "overseers," raised up by the Holy Spirit to "shepherd the church of God." Once again, God's people are seen as a flock of sheep, and the enemy is described as a wolf.

"Be on guard for yourselves and for all the flock..."

He prophetically warned them: Savage wolves would come to the flock, not sparing them. Why? What will be their purpose? Paul says they will draw disciples away from the faith or, one might say, they will devour sheep. And where do the wolves come from? They come "from among your own selves."

The enemy is inside the camp.

If only Satan came to the church as himself. Then we'd have hope. As the New Testament writers said, "Resist the devil and he will flee from you" (James 4:7). But he doesn't always come as himself.

The wolf comes as wolf-sheep. For this reason Paul said emphatically, "Be on guard for yourselves and for all the flock." And again, "Therefore be on the alert." His double warning still flashes like a bright neon sign: *Danger: Wolf-Sheep!*

One might ask, Is the wolf-sheep a New Testament phenomenon? The answer is no. It has been around since the beginning, as far back as the Garden of Eden. Even there, in that sacred, glory-filled land, darkness came dressed as a creature of light. He was wolf-sheep hoping to trap one of God's own. Behold! The enemy was inside the camp, perfectly camouflaged.

Therefore, be on the alert.

The Christian Disguise

I remember our first encounter with a wolf-sheep. It took a long time to spot him. Quite honestly, we knew little about deception in those days. But even when we knew, we didn't want to believe it. Calling someone a "wolf-sheep" sounded so judgmental.

Specifically, we were afraid that we were judging his eternal salvation. Were we calling him Satan in disguise? Were we being unkind, unloving, not forgiving our brother "seventy times seven"? (Matt.18:22).

Erilynne and I were pastoring a church. When this man first came to us, we thought we had a stray, soiled lamb—someone beaten by the world and in need of Jesus Christ and His love. Immediately, the community of faith embraced him with open arms.

Christians are, by definition, a people of love and understanding, ever bearing our heavenly Father's banner of acceptance. Here, we thought, he'll find rest for his sad, tortured soul.

In a short time we noticed this little lamb had a collection of other sheep who followed him wherever he went. Each time he cried, they wiped his tears. When he threatened to return to the outside world, they stood to protect him. Emotionally, they moved to his every whim. His complaints were their complaints, his jealousies were their jealousies. They loved him in Jesus' name.

But they didn't know that he had wrapped them around his little finger. In his display of great need, this helpless lamb was in complete control. None of us knew—until it was too late.

What caught our attention? A dark cloud of heaviness seemed to fall on the congregation. Confusion attended the daily administration of the church. Division was spreading among believers. Heated arguments over insignificant issues kept popping up like little brushfires. The peace of our Lord Jesus Christ was hard to find.

It seemed at every meeting, in every phone conversation—even at quiet social dinners—this one sheep became the topic of discussion. Indirectly and unsolicited, I was informed of his latest problems, his last words, his daily needs. Without doubt, his name had grown mighty in that church.

He had effectively taken our eyes off Jesus.

I had to step in. I called this man and a few of his followers into my office. In a strong yet loving manner, I told him that I was concerned. I reviewed the early days when he first came and the ministry of love that was offered to him. But now, it was clear he was using the people of God. I told him this behavior had to stop. I made specific recommendations that allowed him to continue to receive pastoral care at the church, but it meant that he must stop demanding that his needs be met by those gathered around him.

His reaction was immediate. He stood up, yelled a profane word, and bolted from my office. To my surprise, this man left the church, taking with him his small flock.

Two things happened at once. First, a tangible freedom returned to the church community. We felt the dark cloud of confusion leave. Our hearts were lifted, God's peace returned, and our eyes went back to Jesus. Second, we devoted ourselves to prayer for this group, that they might escape their obsession with this man and return to Christ. We also prayed regularly for the man.

Even to this day, I don't know whether this man was simply a tortured person who happened to gather a following around him or whether it was an intentional act on his part. Still, the outcome was the same. He was our first experience of what wolf-sheep do when they come to the church. He had seductively drawn disciples away. He had so won their hearts that, in the day of confrontation, they all followed him with complete devotion.

We have not forgotten those days, and the scriptural

warning has never left us: "Be on guard for yourselves and for all the flock." It is the job of the church elders to stop division in the name of the Lord Jesus Christ. By so doing, we protect ourselves and the rest of the flock. But, quite honestly, it was hard to confront him. It felt unchristian—as though we were judging this one man. But, we had to ask ourselves, what would have happened if we had not stopped him? How many others would have eventually left?

We learned a hard truth in those days: The Christian disguise is the most difficult disguise of all. This is the first lesson from Eden.

Two

THE WOMAN EVE

E ve was standing within sight of the knowledge tree. For whatever reason, she was alone. Exactly where Adam was, we do not know. God had assigned him the task of cultivating the garden of Eden (Gen. 2:15). Perhaps he was tending to that work.

Also, the immediate presence of the Lord was not there. The writer of this account lets us see "the Lord God walking in the garden" (Gen. 3:8). Obviously, God is everywhere. But that direct physical presence, as described in God walking, enters the story later.

Eve was by herself when the serpent came to her. This fact, coupled with her close proximity to the forbidden tree, allows us to assume the serpent had strategically planned his effort to deceive Eve. He wanted her alone—and near the tree of death.

Why, if I might ask, did the serpent come to Eve alone? Why not the couple together? Or Adam alone? Some commentators have argued that Adam knew the commandment directly from the mouth of God (see Gen. 2:16). Therefore, a deceptive ploy may not have worked with him. But this reasoning falls short. Although Eve came later, she also knew the commandment.

Others have thought: maybe it was easier to deceive the female. But this answer presumes we understand Eve's femaleness. In fact, we don't know if the Eden woman, gloriously handcrafted in God's image, was more open to deception. This also falls short.

What we do know is this: The serpent approached Eve at an opportune time—the couple was separated. This is the real truth. It's the mark of deception throughout all Scripture and remains true today. For deception to work, separation must happen. Someone must be on their own.

For this reason the serpent had to be careful. He knew Eve had instant, direct access to Adam and the Lord. In a moment's notice, she could have cried out, "I'm not sure about this. Let me ask the Lord. Let me ask my husband." Satan had to prevent this move at all costs.

He had to deceive her while she was alone. Any attempt to bring the God-community together would have blown his cover. This could not happen! He had to work—while Eve was still by herself.

He shrewdly waited for just the right moment. Adam was not present. Eve was alone, strolling through Paradise, her lips full of praise to God and her heart rejoicing in the beauty of His creation. Then, as she came to the forbidden tree, a common event happened. A serpent quietly emerged from the brush.

And it began a conversation.

It's the way of deception: Get the sheep alone.

We Belong to Christ and His Community

A New Testament Christian is someone who believes in Jesus Christ as their Savior and Lord. But there's more. A Christian is, by definition, one who belongs to the community. He's no longer a self-centered "I" out on his own. He's joined to an "us" community, a body of people called church.

Jesus identified that "us" in the lost sheep parable. "What man among you," He asked the crowd, "if he has a hundred sheep and has lost one of them, does not leave the ninety-nine in the open pasture, and go after the one which is lost, until he finds it?" (Luke 15:4). That's a simple question in a world of shepherds and sheep.

Everyone knew that shepherds are driven to find lost sheep. Why? Because it is common knowledge that sheep on their own will die. Alone, this animal, whether it knows it or not, has no ability to withstand the forces of nature. Survival is found only under the shepherd's care—and that within a community of other sheep.

So what happens? The shepherd leaves his flock. He is confident of their temporary safety as long as they stay together. Then the shepherd searches for the lone sheep. Once found, "He lays it on his shoulders, rejoicing" (Luke 15:5). Then he brings that one lost sheep home to the ninety-nine.

The same is true for a Christian. The believer has been rescued from the world, the flesh and the devil, saved by our shepherd from the bondage of sin. But salvation does not stop there. Jesus, our shepherd, then hoists us onto His shoulders, rejoicing! And what does he do with us? Where does He take us? To His flock-community, the church. He saves us from sin. Then He saves us from being on our own.

We see this demonstrated at Pentecost, the great outpouring of the Holy Spirit onto the church. Many Christians believe that the Spirit came that day to empower the ministry of the church to the world. And rightly so. He is the power of ministry for us to be witnesses of Jesus Christ to the ends of the earth.

But something else of great importance happened on Pentecost morning. Individual Christians became a "together" community:

> And all those who had believed were together, and had all things in common; and they began selling their property and possessions, and were sharing them with all, as anyone might have need. And day by day continuing with one mind in the temple, and breaking bread from house to house, they were taking their meals together with gladness and sincerity of heart" (Acts 2:44-46).

The believers in the Holy Spirit were a "together" people. Their lives and their possessions now belonged to the Shepherd and His flock. They ate together, worshiped together and lived "day by day ... with one mind" in the fellowship of God and His people.

The key to understanding deception is that it never makes people question their salvation in Jesus. It attacks the community "us" principle. Satan comes to the flock, dressed as a believing sheep, to find one sheep—or a small group of sheep—who will follow him. His mission: to lead them gently away from the shepherd's community.

He is a subtle fox who says, "Let them feel saved! I'll take them out one by one."

The wolf-sheep works at getting sheep to hear his voice. He whispers to a real sheep grazing a few yards away, "You think this grass is good? Have you tried the grass on the other side?" By pure God-talk seduction, these tricksters tickle sheep's ears and "by their smooth and flattering speech they deceive the hearts of the unsuspecting" (Rom. 16:18b). It's that simple.

It's that dangerous. For this reason, the New Testament

epistles uphold a twofold message: First, they sound a loud warning about deceivers; second, they put forth a constant reminder for Christians to remain in the community of faith. Concerning the warning, Paul writes:

> See to it that no one takes you captive through philosophy and empty deception, according to the tradition of men, according to the elementary principles of the world, rather than according to Christ (Col. 2:8).

Deceivers had already come to the Colossae church. They were trying to take them captive with godlike wisdom. But their words were nothing more than philosophy, the tradition of men, and the elementary principles of the world—just empty deception.

Paul says to see to it that deception doesn't happen. His warning to the church is a persistent, ongoing effort to block deceivers.

But that's not the whole message. The second point remains:

> So then you are ... of God's household, having been built upon the foundation of the apostles and prophets, Christ Jesus Himself being the corner stone, in whom the whole building, being fitted together is growing into a holy temple in the Lord; in whom you also are being built together into a dwelling of God in the Spirit (Eph. 2:19-22).

This imagery reveals God as the builder. It is His plan and design that we be connected together in Christ. Therefore, He is in the business of making us His household. By our Father's hand, we are being fitted together into a dwelling of God in the Spirit. This can't happen if believers are on their own.

Paul's words are clear: Christians are a "together" people. We belong to the flock of our shepherd, Jesus. Once we were lost, roaming the countryside and fighting world-battles on our own. But Jesus Christ saved us from all that. He brought us home and placed us into a people—called His church—in the Spirit.

The proclamation of New Testament demands the church of the Lord Jesus Christ be on the alert for deceivers—together! This message, if it's heard and obeyed, stops the serpent of old, for he simply can't get us alone. We have direct access to the Holy Spirit and to the community of faith. We're together![†]

It's hearing that New Testament gospel message that makes us remember Genesis 3, that day when the serpent saw Eve alone. She didn't understand the ways of the devil. She didn't know he comes in disguise. She didn't know he wanted her alone.

And that's exactly what happened. Eve was out on her own.

Never Alone

Story #1: A woman in Pittsburgh received Jesus as Lord at a public rally held by an evangelist passing through town. After he was gone she asked, "Who will help me grow as a Christian?"

She went from church to church, but nothing seemed to satisfy her. She ordered cassette tapes from the evangelist's ministry. She listened to the radio preachers, bought every Christian book under the sun, and studied the Scriptures on her own.

This woman never became part of a Christian fellowship. She sat at home and became a member of the fastest growing denomination in America: the Church of the Alone Christian.

[†] It is possible for groups of believers to fall to the deceiver together. We will examine this later in the book. But the same principle is at work with groups as with individuals. They begin to be isolated from the community of believers. They go out from the church, on their own. The principle of separation is the key to understanding the deceiver's work. When it is truly deception, those separated can no longer dialogue with the Christian community, which upholds the doctrines of New Testament faith.

Story #2: A middle-aged man living outside Washington, D.C., was suddenly jolted by life. Without warning, he was fired from his job. Half an hour later, the phone rang. His son had been rushed to a nearby hospital. The words echoed in his head: "a serious car accident." He called his wife and raced to his son. His only prayer, "Oh, Jesus, don't do this to me."

For the first time in four years, the couple went to church that next Sunday. They prayed together at night, like they used to, and read the Bible in the early morning. They devoted themselves to the Lord Jesus, just as it was when they first received His born-again life some seven years earlier. Each day, they watched their son miraculously recover. Jesus Christ was healing this boy!

Months passed. The man found a better job. Their son had regained his health. The crisis was over. Daily routines began again. In less than six months, the couple had lost their need for Jesus Christ and His community. The pleasures of life became central again. They spent their weekends partying with their friends and not with the Lord and His people. They were back on their own.

Story #3: A minister in Colorado decided to leave his pastorate and begin a nationwide teaching ministry to the church. A few people joined his staff. Today he is an internationally known Bible teacher, but he's accountable to no one. He doesn't belong to a church; there is no flock to minister to this minister.

In his heart of hearts, he trusts nobody. Once he did. Once he belonged to a church where he knew the love, support, and prayer of the body of Christ. But he was hurt, betrayed by Christian brothers. That hurt settled deep in his soul. He vowed he would never be part of the church again. So he set off on his own. He set up his own ministry. He preaches in church after church, and no one realizes he's a lone Christian, a lone sheep. Worse yet, he's a lone overseer. As a preacher, he never expounds the whole gospel. He does not uphold the apostolic witness that demands Christians be flock-bound.

And yet, the gospel is clear. We are to be together, loving each other, wholly aware of how the deceiver works: He gets the sheep alone.

The community-less gospel sells in a free culture like America. It's a country that elevates the constitutional rights of the individual. We are free to do our thing—go where we want to go, be what we want to be. Like the old crooner Frank Sinatra we can boast, "I did it my way!"

Without question, the preaching of the gospel of Jesus has been affected negatively by the American culture. All too often, the preachers only say, "Receive Jesus as your personal Savior!" The message saves lost sheep from sin, but it keeps those same sheep out on their own.

The result is a generation of "solo Christians" who prize Jesus as Lord and yet live life doing their own thing. These believers have not yet been introduced to the warning of Eve in the garden or of the New Testament: Separated sheep, wandering alone, are open prey to the deceiver.

The Scriptures simply don't mesh with the American dream of individual freedom. By definition, a Christian is no longer an "I" but an "us." When we were baptized into Christ Jesus, we were also "by one Spirit … baptized into one body" (1 Cor. 12:13). We are a "together people," a flock-community in Jesus our Shepherd!

As a Christian, you're grafted into "fellowship with us; and indeed our fellowship is with the Father, and with His Son Jesus Christ" (1 John 1:3). Christianity is a new way of life: You become part of God's holy fellowship that speaks in us-language.

Are you standing alone? Has someone whispered in your ear, "You can make it on your own! You don't need a church family. Don't get involved with organized religion. You will just

get hurt. Live for Christ on your own. That's all you need."
Maybe it feels safer to keep yourself independent with the Lord
(plus a few family members, and one or two close friends). But
that is not God's plan for you.

Jesus did not rescue you in the wandering plains of life to
stay out there with you! Yes, He became your personal Savior
and Lord. But He does not stop there. He never does. His
salvation *always* unites us by His Holy Spirit into the fellowship
of believers, His own church, His flock.

If you're out on your own, it's time to let Him pick you up
and place you on His shoulders and carry you to His church
community. Once there, the Holy Spirit will do His great work
of fitting us together into a holy temple of praise to Jesus our
Lord. And we will never be alone.

The time has come to talk about deception. We can no
longer compromise the gospel by preaching a community-less
salvation. It only opens a door for the deceiver, who preys on
lone sheep.

Always remember Eve. If you are out alone, beware! The
wolf knows how to meet you where you least expect him.

Three

THE USE OF GOD'S WORD

The Serpent: "Indeed, has God said, 'You shall not eat from any tree of the garden'?"
The Woman: "From the fruit of the trees of the garden we may eat; but from the fruit of the tree which is in the middle of the garden, God has said, 'You shall not eat from it or touch it, lest you die'" (Gen. 3:1-3).

Thus the conversation began. The serpent asked a question and Eve quite naturally responded. This was an important first step for the serpent. His mission depended on her willingness to talk.

The serpent's question is shocking to us: "Indeed, has God said ... ?" What? Had the serpent come to talk about what God had said? Absolutely. His subject matter was (and always has been) the Word of God. Get the picture: the serpent came to Eve with, figuratively, his Bible open.

God had spoken. He had issued a life-death commandment to the couple: "From any tree of the garden you may eat freely; but from the tree of the knowledge of good and evil you shall not eat, for in the day that you eat from it you shall surely die" (Gen. 2:16-17).

This commandment was a gift of love. When the Lord God made Adam and Eve, He created them in His image and likeness (see Gen. 1:26). They were different from any other living being, for God had breathed His own "breath of life" into them (Gen. 2:7). Their life was His life. Their breath was His breath. They were made in His image.

For this reason, Adam and Eve had to have an opportunity to exercise their will. Since God has the power to choose by His free will, those made in His image also have the power to choose.

The knowledge tree is simply that point of choice.

It was not an evil tree with poisonous fruit! It was a good tree, a perfect tree. But it was set apart by God's love command to be the object of Adam and Eve's choice. They were given the right to decide: Would they love Him, obey His Word, and live forever in His Paradise life? Or would they go out on their own, away from the life of God, into an existence apart from Him?

If they decided to eat the fruit of the knowledge tree, it would mean death. They would break God's commandment and sin. "The wages of sin is death" (Rom. 6:23). So for Adam and Eve, this was a death tree, not because the tree was evil or the fruit poisonous but because it meant disobedience.

In every sense, this Tree of Knowledge was a demonstration of God's holy love. He loved Adam and Eve so much that He did not force their will to love Him back. He gave them the choice! They needed to exercise their God-given choice to love Him—or go out on their own.

The time had come to make the choice. The serpent walked out of the brush with, if you will, his Bible open and a question on his lips. He was ready to discuss the God-commandment. Shrewdly, he acted as though he didn't know what God had said: "Indeed, has God said, 'You shall not eat from any tree of the garden'?" Note the serpent's twisted addition, "any tree?" It was an ignorant question.

But it opened the conversation. It prompted Eve to respond with the words she knew by heart: "God has said, 'You shall not eat from it or touch it, lest you die.'" Her answer was unmistakably clear: There was a forbidden tree, and the consequence of eating its fruit was fatal. Eve added the words *or touch it* to the commandment. It seemed to reinforce that she meant business. She had opted to stay away from the tree.

The serpent's task: Get Eve to eat from the death tree. But how would he do that? Could he get Eve to use her God-given right of choice? Or could he bypass that and wait for Adam—later?

Out came that angel smile. The serpent had a question. Just then, in a manner of speaking, he opened his well-marked, well-read Bible. He wanted to talk about God's Word. It has been the way of deception ever since.

The Biblical Temptation

After his baptism in the Jordan by John, Jesus was led "by the Spirit into the wilderness to be tempted by the devil" (Matt. 4:1). Our Savior stood face-to-face with the prince of this world.

One of the temptations took place in Jerusalem, on the high pinnacle of the temple. There, Satan pulled out his Bible, turned to Psalm 91, and began his conversation with God's holy Word:

If you are the Son of God throw Yourself down; for it is written, "He will give His angels charge concerning You;" and "On their hands they will bear You up, lest You strike Your foot against a stone." Jesus said to him, "On the other hand, it is written, 'You shall not put the Lord your God to the test' " (Matt. 4:6-7).

Psalm 91 is a psalm of faith. It calls the believer to trust the Lord. It assures the faithful, for all time, that the Lord is our security in a time of trouble. No matter what the circumstance, no matter how difficult the situation, He is our shelter.

It upholds God's promise to protect all who cry out to Him, "My refuge and my fortress, My God, in whom I trust" (Ps. 91:2).

Satan quoted the passage, pointed to the ground below, and told Jesus to put His faith to work. If God could be trusted and if Jesus had faith, then He had nothing to worry about. Can't you hear Satan's quiet whisper? "Stand on the promises of God, Jesus. Believe in the Scriptures. Your Father's angels will bear you up. Go ahead, Jesus, jump!" The argument came right from God's Word.

But Jesus didn't accept Satan's invitation. He quoted Deuteronomy 6:16 from memory and said, "On the other hand, it is written ..." His response was brilliant: "Satan, that psalm doesn't apply to this situation. You're dead wrong."

After all, Psalm 91 is meant for the believer who is in adversity. It was not written for the believer to create adversity.

If we create the problem and then ask, "Will God uphold His promises?" we put Him to the test. We question whether God meant what He said. We demand He prove Himself. No wonder Jesus of Nazareth came back, "You shall not put the Lord your God to the test." His words, like a sharp two-edged sword, pierced through the devil's dark logic. For Satan did not want Jesus to step out in faith. No, he wanted Him to step out into sin. Jesus made the right response: "You shall not put the Lord your God to the test."

Satan was wrong. He abused the Scriptures to tempt Jesus into sin. He twisted the Bible for his own purposes. The temptation didn't work. Jesus not only knew the Scriptures—He knew His Father. And that relationship didn't need to be tested.

But one can hardly miss the point. The devil came with his Bible opened, talking about God's holy Word, just as in Eden.

Preaching a Different Gospel

The devil is a Bible preacher.

It's no wonder the New Testament warns Christians about the power of deception. The deceiver slips into our church assemblies and even into our pulpits with his Bible tucked neatly under his arm and a Bible quote on his lips. When he speaks, he speaks about the Scriptures.

For example, Paul was angry when he found out deceivers had upset the Galatian churches. They were stepping out front and center, preaching a different gospel. And nobody was stopping them—until Paul wrote:

> I am amazed that you are so quickly deserting Him who called you by the grace of Christ, for a different gospel; which is really not another; only there are some who are disturbing you, and want to distort the gospel of Christ... Let him be accursed (Gal. 1:6-8).

The young churches in Galatia, birthed by Paul some years before, had already experienced wolves dressed in sheep's clothing. The false brethren looked like real brethren. When they preached in the pulpits, the faithful listened. And why not? They preached from God's holy Word.

But their message was twisted.

They taught the "gospel of Christ." But it was "different"—distorted. Paul wrote to warn them. He bluntly demanded that those disturbers be "accursed." Why? Because Christians were deserting Jesus Christ for the "new gospel" without knowing it. To them, it seemed like God's truth.

Paul wrote to the Galatians for this reason: to stop the spread of deception in the church. It's as if he cried out, "Christians, be alert!" There is a fundamental truth about the deceiver: He preaches Scripture. It is a look-alike gospel. It sounds right. But it is not right. It has the power to lead the church away from Christ.

Just as it was in Eden when the serpent came to Eve, in the wilderness when Satan came to Jesus, and in the church when the deceiver came to Galatia, his well-marked, well-read Bible is open. Even his question is the same: "Indeed, has God said …?" It's the bottom line; he loves to talk about the Word of God. It hasn't changed.

The lesson is a hard one: we can't afford to be naive about this truth. Not everyone who speaks in an endless quotation of Scripture is sent from God. The time has come to be cautious in what we hear—lest we be found deserting the One we love.

The Dynamic Preacher

The devil is an exciting Bible preacher.

Erilynne and I were visiting some relatives in the New England area one summer. On a hot, lazy evening, the phone rang. It was David, a long-time friend. "You've got to come to church with us tonight! There's a famous guest preacher speaking at seven thirty."

We had heard of this preacher and decided to go.

This guy knew the Scriptures! In fifteen minutes, he fired off Bible passages like a machine gun. His personal performance was sensational, dazzling! As I watched the people around me, childlike amazement lit on their faces. As David told me later, "I couldn't believe his knowledge of the Bible. I wish I knew it that well."

But it was more than that. This preacher spoke masterfully, his words carefully chosen. His eloquence, matched with a refined delivery, made each sentence come alive. He was a star performer right out of Hollywood, and I sat bolted to the pew, hanging on his every word.

What explosive charisma! Four times the audience burst into a standing ovation. His real-life experiences touched the depth of my emotions as I found myself laughing and weeping tears, all at the same time. He made me feel as if I knew him, though I was one of eight hundred listeners. The speaker had me in the palm of his hand.

"Do you hear what he's saying?" Erilynne whispered

41

halfway through the sermon. I looked at her, puzzled. I had not been able to touch the substance of his message. The personality was too sparkling, the show too captivating, the eloquence too impressive.

I started listening to the man.

The essence of his talk was the age-old lie: "God helps those who help themselves." He actually said at one point, "Salvation comes to those who are willing to work, willing to love, willing to put in a good deed for the King. For our God blesses only those who pull themselves out of the muck and mire of sin."

This is a gospel that sells. What great news to know that there is something I can do, something I can offer, to be right with God! But it is not the gospel of Jesus Christ. Salvation does not come by our works; as it says in Ephesians 2:8-9, "For by grace you have been saved though faith; and that not of yourselves, it is the gift of God; not as a result of works, that no one should boast."

Martin Luther arose in the sixteenth century to confront this age-old doctrine of works. The Protestant Reformation was birthed because this one man refuted the view that we have something in ourselves to offer the Lord. He preached the message that salvation is God's free gift of grace in Christ. We are justified by faith alone—not by works. The heresy Luther fought against did not disappear. I was listening to it that night: and old message in a new, exciting package.

But who was listening to what this preacher said? It's how he said it! We sat in the congregation awed by the man's gifts, stuck like flies in a spider's web—without knowing it.

After church I overheard people raving about the preacher. No one mentioned the name of the Lord Jesus. No one talked about the content of the sermon. They talked about him, the man. Everyone was enthralled by the superstar's performance.

I would have been too—if Erilynne hadn't urged me to

listen carefully. And I did listen. Behind the preacher's magnetism, I saw the deceiver of old at work. It was the first time I had actually witnessed the devil's gospel behind the Christian mask.

There are many God-sent preachers gifted with a charismatic personality and a mature knowledge of the Scriptures. These men and women, submitted under the direction of the Holy Spirit, minister the gospel—only to the glory of the Lord Jesus Christ.

They are, first and last, His servants. Under His lordship, the gifts of the Spirit are meant to: 1) glorify Jesus, 2) reach out to the unsaved world, and 3) build up His church. Never are these gifts meant for man's own glory. Never! God forbid.

But imagine it. Think about these gifts in the wrong hands. Oh, how easily the deceiver can package the "different" gospel—without the faithful being aware. And, of course, how easy it is for Christians to buy the message simply because they trust the charisma of the dynamic preacher. That godlike charm hides the twisted gospel message.

That night my eyes were opened. Now I knew what Paul felt like the day he wrote to the Galatians. He wanted to protect his brothers and sisters in Christ, so his words had to shock those Christians! By following the new preachers in their church, they were deserting Christ. They neither stood for the gospel of Jesus nor against the false preachers. And they didn't know—they were being deceived.

Two points stand out. First, the Scriptures can be mishandled. Deceivers will come to the present-day church spouting God's Word. They will not handle God's Word accurately. Therefore, Paul wrote to Timothy, his son in the faith, "Be diligent to present yourself approved to God as a workman who does not need to be ashamed, handling accurately the word of truth" (2 Tim. 2:15). It's a question of "handling."

Second, as Christians, we must devote ourselves to the task of knowing God's Word rightly. It is the Holy Spirit's job to guide us "into all the truth" (John 16:13). As we listen to Him, He will train us in the word of truth, that we might be "approved to God." As Christians, joined to the body of Christ, we will discern together when deceivers begin to lead us astray. It is the Holy Spirit who will warn us individually and corporately.

Even with dynamic preachers, we should make it our regular practice to take what we've heard to the Lord in prayer. I thank the Lord for Erilynne, who encouraged me to listen prayerfully that night!

That traveling minister taught me an unforgettable truth: The deceiver is hard to detect. I had naively trusted that I was safe in the Christian church. I could welcome anyone who came with a smile and a well-worn Bible in his hand. But we are not safe.

If the deceiver could break into Eden preaching God's Word, he can break into your world and mine the same way.

Four

THE DENIAL OF GOD'S WORD

The Lord: "You shall surely die" (Gen. 2:17).
The Serpent: "You surely shall not die!" (Gen 3:4).

Satan denied the Word of the Lord. It must have surprised Eve. At first the serpent acted ignorantly, like he didn't know what God had said: "You shall not eat from any tree of the garden?" Eve set the serpent straight: There is a tree called "Disobedience," and disobedience always produces death. This is according to God's own words.

Then, suddenly, the serpent challenged the commandment of God. His naive approach dissolved. In its place a deep well of strength emerged—a new confidence. He no longer appeared confused and distant in his knowledge of God's Word. Instead, the self-assured serpent seemed to know Scripture well enough to contradict it.

The pupil was about to become the teacher.

If he had stopped there, Eve may not have stayed. His statement was too strong on its own. It made God look like a liar. It certainly called His character into question. Eve might have suspected something was wrong. For her to remain, the serpent had to explain his words of denial. More had to be said—quickly.

Before taking another breath, he continued:

> For God knows that in the day you eat from it your eyes will be opened, and you will be like God, knowing good and evil (Gen. 3:5).

Satan immediately disguised the lie. He didn't want this to appear as an overt attack on the character of God. Quite the opposite! He wanted Eve to understand something: He wasn't God's enemy. He was God's special friend—the Lord's favorite pet serpent who had free access to the inner chambers of the throne room. He heard things. He knew things.

The deception was as blinding as the midday sun. Satan presented himself as the Lord's trustworthy comrade, the Almighty's intimate associate, his voice filled with a haughty air of superiority. He behaved like he knew God personally, uniquely.

It's as if he said, "Eve, if you knew what I knew! I've sat in the Lord's inner council. I've been privy to His most secret thoughts. The Holy One has whispered into my ear and spoken confidential information. I know the inside scoop about this knowledge tree! Come here. Let me tell you what God said to me."

His eyes twinkled. He had special knowledge of God. That was his emphasis. He had to get Eve to focus on the knowledge he had—and that she lacked. It was a dangerous moment. Did she trust him? Or would she begin to ask questions? His argument was not tight enough. She could have suddenly asked, "So why is God holding something back from me?" Or she might have reasoned, "If I become more like God, why did He first tell us we would die?" Those questions would have ended the conversation. The serpent had to stress that he had special inside information.

That gave him a certain power—what did he know? What did God say that He didn't tell Adam and Eve? Suddenly, in Eve's world of perfect knowledge, there was something missing. She must have felt a strange void, a blank space. She looked at the serpent. She had no reason to distrust him. And what caught her attention was that he possessed something she didn't have. And that made her curious.

Why? Because the serpent said that God knows the death tree won't make her die. Rather, the tree promised wondrous joy! If she ate the fruit, her eyes would be opened and she would be like God, knowing good and evil. That, said the serpent, was the latest news from the throne room.

And that is how the deceiver works. Since the beginning, he has come to the faithful as God's best friend, someone in the know who wants to share his special knowledge with anyone who will listen.

That so-called inside knowledge of God has a history dating back to the garden. It always denies the Word of the Lord.

The Lie Hidden in Religious Truth

Jesus met the deceiver. Of course, it wasn't like Eden. The deceiver didn't come as a beast of the field. This time he came in the religious robes of the Jewish leaders—dressed as a Pharisee, the spiritual elders of God's people, preachers of His Word.

It didn't work. Jesus didn't buy their smug religious scam. Instead, He took the offensive. He confronted Satan face-to-face. He ripped off the deceiver's mask of holiness and exposed the bloodcurdling nightmare publicly, for all to see. The religious elders were deceivers—children of the devil, dressed in disguise.

He spoke the truth to the Pharisees plainly:

> You are of your father the devil, and you want to do
> the desires of your father. He was a murderer from
> the beginning, and does not stand in the truth,
> because there is no truth in him. Whenever he speaks
> a lie, he speaks from his own nature; for he is a liar,
> and the father of lies (John 8:44).

Jesus wasn't in the wilderness one-on-one with Satan. Nor was He talking to Gentile devil worshipers or Jewish sinners who had strayed from the Law. No, He stood in the Jerusalem temple and addressed the most godly people of His day.

"You are of your father the devil," Jesus told them. "And you want to do the desires of your father." What a confrontation! The pious elders, men of truth, were being called the offspring of the devil—in whom "there is no truth." Liars. Murderers.

How could this be a description of godly religious men?

The Pharisees were zealously devoted to the God of Abraham, Isaac, and Jacob. To them belonged the covenant of circumcision, the Law of Moses, the temple sacrificial system, and all the messianic promises given by the prophets. As Paul once wrote, "I bear them witness that they have a zeal for God" (Rom. 10:2).

The Scriptures were their life. No one knew God's Word like they knew it. For this reason, they were called *Pharisees*, which means "separate ones" or "holy ones." From ancient times, they were separated out by God for a holy life according to His Word.

Pharisees appointed themselves stewards of the sacred writings. Every waking moment was spent rigorously memorizing and following the commandments. The Pharisees lived in fear of not keeping the Scriptures. For this reason, they set up hundreds of new laws, man-made traditions, simply to protect themselves from breaking God's law. If the Lord commanded, "Do it once," they wrote a new tradition saying, "Do it twice—just to be sure!"

The Pharisees had a zeal for God.

But something happened—a great, deceptive switch. Somehow, they had turned their love of God into a love for His Word. That Word was the key to living a righteous life. If they wanted to be more righteous, they needed to devote more of themselves to the Word. They crossed over a dangerous line. Their devotion to His Scriptures became more important than their devotion to Him. The Bible had become an end, not a means—a great means to lead believers into a living relationship with the Lord.

This was idolatry. Those who spent their lives keeping the Law were found guilty of breaking the Law by Jesus Himself:

> You search the Scriptures, because you think that in
> them you have eternal life; and it is these that bear
> witness of Me; and you are unwilling to come to Me,
> that you may have life (John 5:39-40).

The Lord Jesus Christ condemned the Pharisees, for they believed eternal life was found in the Scriptures. They were wrong. The sacred writings point beyond themselves. They hold full authority to bear witness to the living God who works in the here and now. They point to Jesus the Messiah.

But the Pharisees were deceived. The Bible had become their God. This obsession was all too tragic. For the Word they cherished more than life itself now stood in front of them—the Word made flesh, living and breathing, the one named "God with us" who would fulfill the Law and the prophets. And they didn't know Him.

How could this be? The tragedy mounted. The idolatry of God's Word became a breeding ground for pride. The Pharisees took their superior knowledge of Scripture to heart, and they became boastful, overconfident in their knowledge of God. It made them feel special, chosen, as those who are "in" with the Almighty.

It gave them a certain power over the people.

The serpent of old was back with the same old lie: "You can know God deeper than you've ever known Him. You can have a special knowledge that only His chosen ones know—His intimate companions. Possess that knowledge, and you will be like God."

The Pharisees ate from the deceiver's hand. They bought the lie. And just as it was in the garden of Eden, this special inside knowledge of God always denies His Word. But this time it did more than deny God's Word. It crucified Jesus—the very Word of God. The Pharisees sentenced Him to death.

This was no surprise to our Lord. He knew the Pharisees were deceived. He wasn't afraid to confront the "holy ones" to their faces: "You are of your father the devil." But let the truth be known; let it sink deep into our hearts. Jesus' real enemy was not Pontius Pilate or someone from the Roman world-culture. His enemy was in-house—deceivers clothed in the garment of religion who appeared holy, devout, and one with the Lord. These were the ones who nailed the Son of God to the cross.

A Gospel That Tickles

Story #1: A priest in Boston stepped into his pulpit. After a week-long conference debating the theological issues of his denomination, he was tired—tired of fighting the age-old question, "What is truth?" But he was tired mostly of listening to "the hot-headed zealots who hold Scripture as the absolute authority of truth."

"Friends," the priest began, "if I have taught you anything I hope it's this: Truth isn't hard to find. For truth never cares what you believe. It only cares that you love each other."

The priest speaks for many mainline Christians who believe that God's love cannot exclude anyone. That love must embrace the sinner saying, "Let Me love you no matter who you are or what you've done." It's a gospel which doesn't know that God loves the sinner but hates the sin. Therefore they preach, "God doesn't demand that you repent of sin and be 'born again' to Jesus Christ. He loves you as you are. You don't have to believe anything. You are promised heaven when you die. You're not going to burn in hell."

They preach God's understanding love. They aren't concerned with either "strange doctrines" (1 Tim. 1:3) or "sound doctrine" (1 Tim. 4:6). Their gospel doesn't demand radical repentance from sin and conversion to Jesus Christ. It can't. It can never require choice, for those who choose wrongly must have a place in God's eternal kingdom. That is their definition of God's love.

When this message is preached by bishops and ministers, it sounds godly. It carries the authority of God and His Word to the people. But it is not the living gospel the Almighty God and Father entrusted to His church. It's a man-made version—a deceptive half-truth. These people are denying the Word of the Lord.

Story #2: In the midwest a church had grown to five thousand members in eight years. The pastor started with nightly meetings in his basement while working a full-time job. Today the church broadcasts on radio and television, reaching thirty-five cities coast to coast.

In a television interview the pastor was asked, "What would you tell struggling ministers?" He replied, "The message I preach is this: 'God loves you. Jesus died for you. Jesus loves you just the way you are!' That message is the backbone of my ministry and the reason for the church's success. Ministers, preach that word!"

What could be wrong? The church is growing. The Bible is at the heart of the community. The pastor is a dynamic, motivational preacher. Christians nationwide are being attracted to this man.

Here's the problem: he preaches a "teddy bear" gospel.

Each Sunday he injects a warm, comfortable message into

the veins of his congregation. His charming delivery and soft, velvet voice somehow make life manageable again. People feel good about themselves, their jobs, their world. Their stressed lives, full of despair, turn to the promise of hope. Success is possible in the impossibilities of life. His positive message is like a cup of hot chocolate on a wintry afternoon.

It's a teddy bear gospel that never requires conversion. It does not lead sinners to the Cross: "And he who does not take his cross and follow after Me is not worthy of Me" (Matt. 10:38). Even though this man preaches that God's love is expressed in Jesus' death on the cross, nothing is demanded of the listener—not repentance, not a changed life, not a decision to follow Jesus into His death.

This pastor denies God's Word. He made a decision to preach the gospel that sells, not the gospel that changes lives through costly repentance and true faith in the Lord Jesus Christ. Unfortunately, many ministers have followed this pastor's example. In the mid-1990s churches have sprung up all over the country that draw crowds, entertain them, make them feel good about their lives, and send them home with a smile. The success of bringing people to their churches has become more important than preaching the whole costly message of the gospel.

Without question, it's hard to hear "the lie," especially when that lie tickles our ears and tricks our eyes. How can we see the lie when it comes from religious leaders? Oh how easily impressed we are by people who seem to know God better than we do! Maybe they are ordained pastors. Maybe they have known Christ longer or know the Scriptures better or see heavenly visions or appear on television.

We must watch out! We must ask the question, "Are they sent by the Lord Jesus Christ?" For no matter what the mask looks like, the deceiver always comes as someone in the know. He has special knowledge. He's got an insider's wisdom that seems God-inspired—but it isn't.

"O Timothy," Paul wrote, "guard what has been entrusted to you, avoiding worldly and empty chatter and the opposing arguments of what is falsely called 'knowledge'" (1 Tim. 6:20).

The time has come to stand in the truth and "guard what has been entrusted" to us. For this is the truth: The deceiver comes to the church of Jesus Christ with his Bible opened and a special revelation direct from the mouth of God to share with you and me.

He has a knowledge that always denies the Word of the Lord.

Five

TO BE LIKE GOD

The words echoed inside her head: "Your eyes will be opened, and you will be like God, knowing good and evil." There she stood, directly in front of the "knowledge" tree. She stared at it, her eyes fixed on its lush green boughs filled with golden, ripe fruit. It was the first time Eve had taken a good look.

The serpent had stepped back. He would never speak to Eve again. He had taken his one, best shot. There was nothing more he could do. Eve had to operate her God-given right of choice alone. But what kind of choice had the serpent given her?

She could remain as she was—or eat, and experience a deeper relationship with the Lord. This was not a decision between good and evil, life with God and life outside of God, a tree of death and a Tree of Life. This was not like the moment when Elijah the prophet called his generation to choose between serving the Lord and serving the foreign god Baal. The serpent made her think this was a choice between good and glorious!

His last words were like pieces of chocolate laced with a hidden poison. It was all a deceptive lie: "You will be like God." She would not be like God. If she ate from the death tree, she would die.

It was a lie because Adam and Eve were already like God. They were the only part of God's creation to be made in His image and likeness. He created them as finite copies of His infinite person. So God, who is love, created perfect man and woman to bear the exact imprint of His love. They were in His image! They were like Him.

Everything Eve needed to be like God was already inside her. But the deceiver, by his special knowledge, had led her to believe otherwise. According to the serpent, God had withheld information; namely, the knowledge of good and evil. Her eyes were not truly opened. She was not completely "like God"— yet. She lacked what the knowledge tree could offer. She needed to eat.

This liar spoke: "You [are] not like God. But you [will be] if you eat." Suddenly, there was something Eve had to do. And when she did it, she would be like God.

The lie went on: If she ate, she would know good and evil like God knows it. Sure, God knew *about* evil! But it was a lie that God knew evil by experience. If Eve ate from the death tree, she would experience evil firsthand! That was not like God.

Eve was being tricked. She looked at the death tree through the eyes of the deceiver. Only then did she see a tree that would make her more like God. And what, she reasoned, could be wrong with that? To eat would please her Lord and God. Her eyes, closed to this special God-knowledge, would be opened—just like His!

The serpent's work was over. Eve had to make a decision.

The Heart of Sin

Eve could not feel the venom in the serpent's words: "You will be like God." Deception had masked the evil and transformed it into an opportunity for Eve to grow closer to the Lord.

These words define the very nature and condition of sin. They describe the evil desire of Satan himself. We know that Satan was originally made with "the seal of perfection, full of wisdom and perfect in beauty." He was an angelic being, an "anointed cherub" (Ezek. 28:12, 14), created by God and called "very good" (Gen. 1:31).

But Satan sinned. Theologians disagree over the exact time of Satan's downfall. We join those who believe it happened at some point after the creation and before the serpent's arrival in Eden. It was then that the glorious cherub was cast down from heaven, an event Jesus Himself witnessed: "I was watching Satan fall from heaven like lightning" (Luke 10:18).

What was his sin? Why did the great angel fall from grace? Isaiah captured the wickedness that seared Satan's heart:

But you said in your heart, "I will ascend to heaven; I will raise my throne above the stars of God, and I will sit on the mount of assembly in the recesses of the north. I will ascend above the heights of the clouds; I will make myself like the Most High" (Isa. 14:13-14).

Five times in this passage Satan said, "I will." Sin never focuses on God but on self—the great "I." Satan wanted his "throne" to ascend above heaven, above the angels, even above God Himself. Oozing with self-pride, he wanted to taste the divine power, the glory. If only he could be worshiped as God alone is worshiped.

"I will make myself like the Most High." This was Satan's sin. We see it again at Jesus' temptation. He wanted Jesus to "fall down and worship" him (Matt. 4:9). He still wanted to reach for the Almighty's throne and experience real God-likeness. How better to achieve this than by having the eternal Son of God bow down and worship him?

It's also the sin found in mankind after the fall. The sin-filled creature wants to be number one, center stage. The great "I" seeks to be God, to have power, to be in control, to have a lasting name, to be adored by others greater than ourselves, to reign as king over our little kingdoms. It's a me-centered world.

It's our pursuit of self loving self, not self loving God. This is the fallen human condition. But let's remember this one important point: Satan's sin-driven desire—"I will make myself like the Most High"—became a religious deception to Eve. The serpent marketed his evil desire as a living desire for God. Sin no longer looked sinful. It was adorned in religious garments and in godly humility. It piously asked, "Doesn't God want us to be like Him?"

That's always the question of the devil dressed in light. And with it comes something for us to do. Some action must be taken—to eat a piece of garden fruit or to fall down and worship. The devil always calls us to act in order to receive the promised likeness of God.

Casting a Spell in Galatia

The apostle Paul put forth the gospel of Jesus Christ in one sentence:

> I have been crucified with Christ; and it is no longer
> I who live, but Christ lives in me; and the life which
> I now live in the flesh I live by faith in the Son of
> God, who loved me, and delivered Himself up for me
> (Gal. 2:20).

The heart of the Christian faith declares that when the Son

of Man died on the cross of Calvary for our sins, we also died. We were crucified with Christ. When we believe in Christ's atoning death and receive the forgiveness of our sin, He gives us the great gift of new, everlasting life. In His resurrection, we are resurrected. Like Paul, we testify, "It is no longer I who live, but Christ lives in me."

That is the gospel. God the Father loves us. He sent His Son to die on our behalf. And now God, the Holy Spirit, has come to empower our lives from within. To be a Christian means we have died with Christ, we are born again by His Spirit, and the King of Kings lives in us!

The deceiver works against this good news. He tries to convince believers that having "Christ in you, the hope of glory" (Col. 1:27) is not enough. There is more to the Christian life. There is something else we must do to be real Christians—more to do.

This was the lie that infiltrated the Galatian churches. It was the reason Paul wrote to the Galatians. It was his job to stop the deceivers and prevent Christians from believing that ancient lie:

O You dear idiots of Galatia, who saw Jesus Christ
the crucified so plainly, who has been casting a spell
over you? I will ask you one simple question: did you
receive the Spirit by trying to keep the Law or by
believing the message of the Gospel? Surely you
can't be so stupid" (Gal. 3:1-3, J.B. Phillips).

The deceivers came casting a spell. These were Jewish converts to Christ who wanted to remain faithful to Judaism. To them, salvation in Jesus could not forsake the sacred Jewish traditions.

Their teaching demanded that Christians do more than believe in Christ; obedient followers must also keep the Law.

First, they upheld the rite of circumcision. Believers since Abraham, including our Lord, were circumcised as a perpetual sign of God's covenant. In their minds, the coming of the

Messiah would not nullify this God-given rite. It must continue—as always.

Second, the entire Law of Moses must be observed as a daily practice. Without faithful obedience to the commandments, salvation was not possible (see Acts 15:1). Third, at all costs, Gentile Christians must not mingle with Jewish Christians. The Gentiles remained different, unclean.

Their list of rules was meant to have equal weight with the new gospel. Who could possibly offer an argument against obeying the Law and tradition? It sounded right. It seemed to offer the right mixture of God's work in the Old Testament and His present work in Christ.

In fact, many of the apostles bought the message. For example, James (the brother of our Lord Jesus and the first bishop of Jerusalem) fell captive to this doctrine. He even blessed these false teachers and sent them out as missionaries to the young churches! Later, in Antioch, Peter and Barnabas would also succumb to this new gospel (see Gal. 2:11-13).

Their deceptive spell spread like a deadly cancer.

Paul called the Galatians "idiots ... stupid." They had traded the true gospel for a counterfeit. For the serpent-lie said: "Believers, you are not (present tense) pleasing to God. But you will be (future tense) if you follow our long list of rules." It taught that belief in Jesus Christ and His saving work on Calvary wasn't enough. There was more to do.

Their message denied the gospel. Anyone who has put their whole trust in the sacrificial, atoning death of Jesus Christ and His resurrection *is* (present tense!) pleasing to God. As Christians, we have received this great salvation by faith—not by works. There is nothing we can do to earn His saving grace. Being justified by His grace, not by our righteous works, means we have nothing more to do to be accepted by our Father in heaven. Anyone who says differently, says Paul, is casting a spell.

The Galatian deception has its roots in Eden. Look at the parallel: The serpent tried to convince Eve (the Galatians) that being in God's image (being in Christ) was not enough. The knowledge tree (the list of rules) would add to her (their) relationship with God and make her (them) more like Him. The deceiver hasn't changed.

He tricked Eve. He tricked the most eminent apostles of the early church. And he's at work today. His lie—"Do this and you will be like God"—holds one promise. It always leads to death.

You Will Be Like Jesus

Erilynne and I finished a preaching mission in Southport, Connecticut, in the late spring of 1985. After the last Sunday service, the pastor invited us to have lunch with him and an old friend. We were both surprised to meet Glen Scott Bailey and his new wife.

Glen was one of the most sought-after preachers in the evangelical movement of the late sixties. He pastored a large church in the suburbs of New York City. He was twenty-two years in the pastorate. He had an engaging preaching style, which made him a draw on the speaking circuit. His books sold well. Christian magazines covered him regularly. So when the scandal broke, it was known throughout most of the Christian community.

We had heard only the basic story: He had an affair, divorced his wife, left the ministry, married his lover, and became a real estate broker somewhere in Delaware. We were stunned, to say the least, to be sitting across the dining room table from this famous fallen preacher we had never met but knew a great deal about.

Quite honestly, the first half of the luncheon was devoted to dodging the scandalous issue. It finally surfaced when Glen introduced the subject. It seemed as though he was still wrestling with the deeper questions of his faith. It didn't take long for us to learn that the scandal, which on the surface seemed to be rooted in lust, had its roots embedded in a fundamental theological question: How do we deal with sin as Christians?

Beneath his dynamic personality, Glen struggled with his bent toward sin. On the preaching circuit, he was an evangelist calling for people to repent of their sin and come to Christ. But in his church, he was a pastor and teacher. To his credit, he knew the New Testament doctrine of sanctification. He knew the Holy Spirit had been given to be the power, the source, for us to face the temptations of sin. He wrote Philippians 2:12-13 in his mind and on his heart: "Work out your salvation with fear and trembling; for it is God who is at work in you, both to will and to work for His good pleasure." In principle, he knew that believers face the power of the world, flesh, and devil every day. And he knew the secret: The Lord promises to be "at work in you."

But Glen was not able to live in this truth. Instead of depending on the daily grace of the Holy Spirit to work in his life, he formed a doctrine of legalism for himself, his family, and his church. He rigorously put rules forward. He hoped these rules would prevent him and his congregation from falling into sin's powerful grasp. The more sin knocked at his door, the longer the list of rules became. And, as Senior Pastor, Glen enforced these rules with strict discipline.

For Glen and his peers in the church, legalism was birthed out of a born-again, living relationship with Jesus Christ. The reason they turned to the list of rules was altogether positive. They wanted to be like Christ and to live godly, holy, righteous lives in a pagan world. The rules would help safeguard their journey. It would protect them from the devil's temptations. In their minds, it was completely motivated by the noble desire to please the Lord and be like Him.

So the list of rules began: no drinking, no smoking, no swearing, no movies, no dancing, no recreational activities with non-Christians, no feeble excuses for missing Sunday and weekday church services, and women must not wear slacks, unbecoming makeup, short skirts, or anything that might appear provocative—the list went on. There were separate lists for men and their conduct at work, for the behavior of men and women in Christian marriage, and for Christian dating. For example, unmarried couples were not permitted to hold hands until after marriage.

Glen Scott Bailey pastored and policed his congregation. There was a high degree of accountability among the elders and with the people. Stories circulated periodically through the church when an elder failed to meet the standards. Actual declarations were made at the Sunday morning services when a member of the congregation defiantly rebelled against one of the rules. It was normal, on occasion, to hear that someone or some family had been excommunicated from the church. Everyone knew the rules—and the consequences for breaking them.

There was a strong, godly desire motivating Glen. He was fighting with the power of sin in his life. He truly felt that these rules would provide the necessary shield to protect him, his family, and his church from worldly influences and the crafty schemes of the devil. He sincerely believed that this method— if practiced faithfully—would make their lives more like that of Jesus Christ.

Glen wanted to be like Jesus.

But slowly his gospel—the age-old gospel of works— failed. It took time. Unfortunately, there were no great apostles to confront Glen as Paul confronted the churches of Galatia. No one stopped him by saying, "I will ask you one simple question: Did you receive the Spirit by trying to keep the Law or by believing the message of the gospel?" It took years before Glen realized that the Christian life cannot be lived under the strict discipline of the law.

The first sign Glen missed. His own contemporaries, who came to faith at the same time and helped found the church, could not keep the demanding expectations of the pastor's rules. One by one, over time, the first generation of elders drifted away from the church and Glen's life. As hard as it was to experience the loss each time a "founding family" left, Glen never understood why. He never stopped to consider the fundamental reasons why his peers could not stay.

The second sign undid the famous preacher. After two decades in the church, the born-again pastor had raised up a new generation. The infants had become young men and women. His own children were raised in those very same Sunday school classes. As these teenagers graduated from high school and went their own way, very few returned to the church—or any church, for that matter. As soon as they could, they fled their pastor, their parents, and the harsh rules of Christianity.

From infancy, they understood the Christian faith as a discipline of following rules. Being a Christian meant behaving, doing everything right, memorizing Scripture, staying away from certain people, and being different from everybody else. Their parents' lives never demonstrated that eternal life is a free gift of God's grace in Christ. All they saw in their elders was constant obedience to church laws. These kids knew one gospel message: Salvation was by works—not by grace through faith in the Son of God.

This generation came not to a living relationship with the Savior of the world but only to rules.

It was a different story for their parents. They came into a relationship with Christ and experienced new life in Him. Then they made the rules. Their children got only the rules. By the time they grew up, a high percentage of kids bolted from under the heavy bondage of legalistic Christianity. Many parents lost their teens to the free, lawless, immoral life-style of the American culture. Near the end of Glen's pastorate, stories went around the church of high-profile families who lost their teens to the pagan world. These stories moved and disturbed Glen's soul deeply.

His gospel failed once and for all the night Glen's son was arrested for selling drugs. Worse yet, while at the prison Glen met his son's pregnant lover. The pastor-father lost his temper. He demanded to know why his son had failed Christ. The more he yelled, the harder his son's face became. In desperation, Glen ran from the prison and drove off. His family searched for him for ten days. The preacher's world came crashing down. He had lost his son. He had lost a whole generation of children who were now facing the world by his Christian rules. And they would fail as his son had failed. As he had failed.

He came back and resigned his pastorate.

That night at the prison, everything Glen had built over twenty-two years of ministry was wiped out. In a depressed state, his demise led him to draw certain conclusions: There was no way to protect himself from the power of sin. His legalistic method had failed. Therefore, he reasoned, there is no way to live a righteous, godly life here on earth. The flesh is simply unable to resist the lusts of the world, the flesh, and the devil.

Rather than fight sin, why not give in and embrace it? With his whole world crumbling before him, Glen left his wife, moved to Delaware, studied real estate, moved in with a woman, and eventually married her. Glen Scott Bailey started a new life.

That Sunday afternoon, the once-famous preacher told us his story. At first, we thought he was still searching for answers. But it soon became clear that he had stopped searching. He wanted us to feel the pain of his journey, to hear his unanswerable questions, and then—to shock us with his inevitable conclusion. He sat at the edge of his chair, as if waiting to see our reaction as he summed up the futility of being a Christian, let alone a preacher of the gospel.

"You know," he said, the bitterness etched into his face, "God is a big tease. He gives you a glimpse of His glory. You can see it. You want to do everything in your power to live for Him and be like Him. But you can't. He abandons you. He doesn't give you the ability to fight the powers of hell on earth. There's nothing you can do but give in to the devil. Then, when this life is over, you just pray God in His mercy will take you home. He is a tease! The gospel is a tease!"

As we left the pastor's home that afternoon, Erilynne and I wondered how it all began. At some point in Glen's life, he must have met someone. Perhaps it was someone of influence or an older pastor he respected. The words whispered in his ear were the same Eve heard in the garden of Eden: "You know, there is something you must do if you want to be more like God." And Glen took the words to heart. He needed to keep himself from succumbing to the dark powers of this world. So the list of rules began to form. Slowly, without his knowing it, he exchanged the life-giving gospel of grace for the ancient, deadly gospel of works.

If only Glen had fallen on his face in his day of demise and prayed to the Lord, "Show me thy truth!" Then he would have known the free grace of God's forgiving love—just as he knew it the first day he received Christ as his Savior. He would have known by experience the power available in the Holy Spirit to live the Christian life. And what a witness he could have been to the Christian world, passionately refuting the ancient lie that had poisoned his preaching for so many years. But he did not turn to the Lord. His eyes were fixed—all he could see was his son's face, his cold, blank eyes staring through the prison bars at his great preacher dad.

Glen Scott Bailey gave up the race and fled into the arms of sin. If only he had remembered Eve.[†]

[†]In the years following, Glen Scott Bailey found sanctuary under the ministry of caring pastors who nurtured him back into the fellowship of the church. He never returned to the pastorate, but he has recognized the heresy rooted in legalistic Christianity, and his season in the embrace of sin is over.

Six

AFTER THE MIND

The serpent escaped back into the brush. Turning toward the woman one last time, his eyes beamed with a dark, gloating pride. "Success!" his heart whispered as Eve reached for the fruit of disobedience. With any luck, he'd have them both by nightfall.

He was as phony as a three-dollar bill. But the masquerade had worked. The master magician had pulled the right trick out of his little black bag. He had teased her mind into seeing what's not really there. And it worked! She watched—and believed.

That's real magic.

Everything had gone according to plan. The serpent costume had done its job, changing the prince of darkness into a creature of Eden light. It made a good first impression, and that's always the trademark of a good salesman. It got his foot in the door.

The conversation went smoothly. Eve suspected nothing. She quite naturally talked about the Lord and His Word. This was a good sign. It allowed the serpent to press on. He introduced his special status: He had knowledge. He was in with the Almighty. He had heard secrets and felt it was his duty to come to her as an official ambassador of truth. She bought it, and the serpent was on a roll.

There was one last trick, a final great moment. He had some exclusive bits of gossip from the mouth of God. Would she listen? Did she want to know this was the Tree of Knowledge, not a death tree? It had the power to make her like God—just in the eating. And what's more, he didn't say it, but he seemed to imply that the Lord would bless her in the eating.

The trickster-magician knew the secret art of deception—to play tricks with the mind. That was his goal. He was not an Eden serpent. He was not a special confidant of the Lord. Eating the forbidden fruit wasn't God's plan. But the devil is a magician, a stage performer acting his part to perfection. And he wanted Eve in his kingdom. If he had her, could Adam be far behind?

Before he vanished from sight, he knew. His one best shot had worked. He had deceived the woman into believing that hell's lie was God's truth. And that was that. From that time on Satan was and always would be "the deceiver." Why not? He knew how to do it—just get the mind and lead it simply, gently astray.

A Blessing to the Disguised

In Jacob's early life he had a reputation for being a deceiver. His name means "one who supplants." When he entered God's covenant, the Lord changed his name to Israel. But before that time, Jacob knew how to deceive. In Jacob's deception of his father, for example, we find the attack on the mind as the dominant scriptural principle. Without question, deception is an illusion of the mind!

Isaac was old. His eyes were blind, and his body was wasting away. The miracle child of Abraham and Sarah was at death's door. Knowing this, Isaac called for Esau, his firstborn son. The traditions must be kept: Before he died, Isaac had to pass on the covenant blessing of God to the eldest son. So he called Esau to his side.

He sent him out to hunt game and prepare a "savory dish for me such as I love, and bring it to me that I may eat, so that my soul may bless you before I die" (Gen. 27:4). Esau had longed for this blessing and went out at once as his father commanded.

When Rebekah, Isaac's wife, overheard this conversation, she was furious. She had another plan! She acted quickly. While Esau was out hunting, she slaughtered one of their own livestock and prepared a mouthwatering meal. Then she called for Jacob, the second-born son. Was it possible? Would it work? Could Jacob take the meal in, deceive his father, and walk out with the blessing?

It was worth a try. But there were problems. Jacob wasn't a hairy man like his brother, Esau, and this got Jacob worried:

> Behold, Esau my brother is a hairy man and I am a smooth man. Perhaps my father will feel me, then I shall be as a deceiver in his sight; and I shall bring upon myself a curse and not a blessing (Gen 27:11b-12).

Mother wasn't worried. Jacob put on his brother's clothes so that he smelled just like Esau, the man of the fields. He also wore animal skins on his hands and on the back of his neck. Now he was as hairy as Esau. With that, Jacob entered the room where his dim-sighted father lay. He set the covenant meal before him.

Jacob spoke first. "My father ... I am Esau your first-born;

I have done as you told me. Get up, please, sit and eat of my game, that you may bless me" (Gen. 27:18a-19). Instantly, Isaac was confused. This wasn't the voice of Esau! It was his son Jacob.

"Please come close," Isaac responded, "that I may feel you, my son, whether you are really my son Esau or not" (Gen. 27:21). The disguised hairy hands worked. Father questioned his son again, "Are you really my son Esau?"

Jacob replied, "I am" (Gen. 27:24).

Isaac tested his son once more.

"Please come close and kiss me, my son" (Gen. 27:26). His large hand wrapped around the back of his son's neck. Hair! Yes, it felt like Esau. But more, the smell wasn't Jacob's. His younger son had grown up in Rebekah's footsteps, never wandering beyond the gates of the house. This was the smell of a rugged outdoorsman. This was Esau.

The matter was closed. Isaac was convinced. He ate his meal and drank his wine. After dinner he laid his hands on the head of his firstborn son Esau (or so he thought) and blessed him.

Isaac did not know he was deceived until the real Esau came into his room with the covenant meal later that night. In those days and in God's eyes, a blessing was eternal. It could not be revoked. "Your brother," Isaac said matter-of-factly, "came deceitfully, and has taken away your blessing" (Gen. 27:35). The news utterly destroyed Esau.

Rebekah and Jacob had done their work well. Isaac truly believed he was blessing Esau. Was it the garment that smelled like Esau? Was it the hairy hands and neck? Or was it a father's trust in his two sons, a trust that only knows honesty and not deceit?

No matter; he was deceived. His mind was gently led astray from the truth. He really thought he was blessing his eldest son.

The Magician and the Church

Let "no advantage be taken of us by Satan" Paul wrote, "for we are not ignorant of his schemes" (2 Cor. 2:11). Paul was writing the Corinthians—again. The church was under siege—not by Satan and his dark dominions attacking from the outside. He was inside, dressed as the serpent-magician, working his old magic.

Paul saw through their disguise. It was his job to tell the Corinthians, "Those new preachers in your church are not sent from the Lord Jesus Christ!" He told the truth: Deceivers had come.

> For such men are false apostles, deceitful workers, disguising themselves as apostles of Christ. And no wonder, for even Satan disguises himself as an angel of light (2 Cor. 11:13-14).

Paul knew Genesis 3 all too well. The deceptive mind game has always begun by perfecting the disguise. That's why Satan came as a serpent in Eden. It's why he comes to the church as an apostle of Christ—even "an angel of light." The routine hasn't changed.

Then comes the second step. The false apostles entice their listeners with God-talk. They distort the truths of Scripture, and with their endless arguments they try to capture the faithful:

> For if one comes and preaches another Jesus whom we have not preached, or you receive a different spirit which you have not received, or a different gospel ... (2 Cor. 11:4).

It was all counterfeit. They did not preach the Lord Jesus Christ but "another Jesus." Nor did they experience the Holy Spirit of Pentecost, but a "different spirit." Theirs was a "different gospel" and not the true gospel entrusted to us by our ascended and reigning Lord.

It was Eden revisited. The serpent in Genesis 3 preached about "another" God. His God had withheld information from

Eve. His God secretly wanted the woman to eat from the knowledge tree. And his God was love; He would never condemn her for eating a piece of the fruit. Satan's god is always a look-alike God.

Paul feared for the Corinthians. Before the deceivers attempted the third and final step, the act of tricking the Corinthians into acts of disobedience, Paul wrote them. He demanded they remember Genesis 3, the woman Eve, and the serpent-magician who played his tricks and stole her mind away:

> But I am afraid, lest as the serpent deceived Eve by his craftiness, your minds should be led astray from the simplicity and purity of devotion to Christ (2 Cor. 11:3).

It was time for the Corinthians to learn the secret of Genesis 3, for the footprints of the deceiver were now in their church. And, as we have learned from that Eden experience, those godlike footprints lead straight into the pit of hell.

A Parable on I-95

Erilynne and I landed at La Guardia, loaded our luggage into the car, and drove from the New York City airport to our Connecticut home. It was a burning, hazy summer afternoon.

We crossed the Whitestone Bridge and rode some twelve miles before seeing the traffic slow and finally stop. Orange road construction signs appeared everywhere. The two right lanes were closed. The signs instructed us to merge into one left lane.

That took an hour. I thought that once we merged left, it would be smooth sailing. No such chance. We inched our way down I-95, crawling like a lazy tortoise. Such frustration! We saw many cars off the road that day, hoods up, with angry travelers helplessly staring into the steaming white smoke of an overheated engine.

There we sat, our windows down, dripping with sweat,

when I noticed something strange in my rearview mirror. The guy behind us was pounding his dashboard with his fists in red-hot anger. He had clearly come to the end of his patience.

Then he started blowing his horn at us; I couldn't believe it. What was I supposed to do? His head came out of the window, and he was swearing, demanding the traffic in front of him to move! Of course, we didn't. We couldn't. With that, the man crossed between the orange cones, drove into the forbidden middle lane, and took off.

"Look at that!" I shouted. "What's that guy doing?" But that wasn't all. In mind-boggled shock, I watched the car behind him also jump into the middle lane. Then the next car... and the next ... and the next ... until a steady stream of cars flowed naturally behind us, each into the forbidden lane.

"Where do they think they are going?" I asked absolutely dumbfounded.

At some point, the traffic came to a dead stop. There was a whole new middle lane full of cars with no place to go—except to merge left—as we had done once before. We were there nearly three hours. The volcanic anger of this one man had led to untold misery for thousands of exhausted people.

"Unbelievable!" I croaked. "How can people be that stupid?"

"You can't blame them," Erilynne said, "most of those people didn't know what they were doing. They were tricked. They saw the car ahead of them move and thought, 'Hey, we're moving. Finally! Let's go!' How were they to know they were following a madman?"

"The second driver knew," I said. "He heard the horn blowing and watched that guy throw a fit. He had to know it was wrong."

"Yes, it is possible the third and fourth drivers knew too," she continued. "But what about all the others? What about that family you saw with all the children? They were probably praying for the traffic to move. Suddenly, they saw the car in front of them moving. How would you feel? 'Praise God! The waiting is over! Thank you Lord for answered prayer and caring for our children!'"

"So they were just duped," I said.

"Sure. They sped into the middle lane not knowing it was a trap—a big trick pulled by a guy who lost his temper."

I have never forgotten that story. It is the way of deception. Since the beginning, Satan has known how to lead Christians into the forbidden middle lane. He comes to the faithful dressed in the religious garb of a charismatic preacher or a trustworthy pastor. He speaks of Jesus Christ, quotes Scripture, and lets us know we can trust him to lead us safely onward.

How many blindly follow, not knowing Satan is the greatest magician, tricking the mind into disobedience and forbidden lanes?

A cold bitter chill washed down my back as I sat in the car that day. I had seen everything: the man's anger, his decision to break the law, the choice of the first few drivers to follow him, and then the deception of hundreds who trespassed unknowingly.

And what did I do? Nothing. I sat back and watched.

"No more!" I vowed. "That won't happen again. I'll jump out of my car and wave my hands shouting, 'Stop! You're following a madman!' It has to be done. Someone must stand on the side of the road and give warning." That's what Paul did for the Corinthians. It's exactly what must be done for the church in our generation.

Part II

THE ATTRACTION

Seven

GOOD FOR FOOD

"When the woman saw that the tree was good for food ..." (Gen. 3:6).

Eve had never known need for food before. From the moment she opened her eyes, Eve was in the presence of the Lord. She was sinless and free, "naked ... and not ashamed" (Gen. 2:25).

In every sense of the word, she was complete. Her Eden home was adorned in perfection, from the fresh, cool streams watering the garden to the stars sparkling under the unending canopy of a bright, glory-filled universe. United in love to her husband, walking face-to-face with her Lord, Eve lived in the paradise of God's love that neither knew need nor the longing of need.

That completeness began inside. Eve was joined to the

Lord, filled with His life and love. She was in His image. Her breath, which came first from Adam, originated in God. His own glory was inside her and she knew it, the very life source of her being.

They were in Him. He was in them. Just as Jesus would later describe true kingdom living: "Even as Thou, Father, art in Me, and I in Thee, that they also may be in Us" (John 17:21). This was Eden: God and man joined as one with His love uniting them at the center.

But somehow it happened. It was the first time. Standing in front of the knowledge tree, Eve felt the longing pangs of need.

The serpent salesman had made his pitch. He knew the key to good advertising. If there isn't a need for the product, create the need. How? By convincing Eve there was something missing in her perfect life: She didn't have the knowledge of good and evil.

The sales presentation was concise and inviting: 1) God had this knowledge, 2) it was possible for her to have it too, and 3) she could *really* be like God. But for this to work she must do something: *eat!*

Eve had seen the tree before, but it held no attraction. It spelled rebellion to God's commandment. She had God's eyes then, and the love inside her heart would never long for anything displeasing to God.

But things had changed. She saw the tree with serpent-eyes, through the glasses of his deceptive logic. Suddenly, it possessed a knowledge of God she didn't have—and now wanted. It had power to make her more like God, someone more pleasing to Him.

Eve felt desire.

As she curiously gazed at the tree, touching the God-shaped fruit, she saw that it was "good for food." What tree wasn't good for food? All of Eden was bursting with fruit trees, God's best cuisine. It didn't matter. She had different eyes now.

Her mouth watered for the taste. She wanted to eat. Without doubt, her real appetite (how well she knew!) was to be like God. Oh, what sweet pleasure! As she studied the boughs decorated with luscious fruit, it seemed to satisfy this new need inside her. Yes, she realized with surprise, it does look good for food.

Seek First His Kingdom

The blood of Abel was still fresh on Cain's hands when Adam and Eve learned the news: Their second son was dead. Grief burned hot in their hearts like a consuming fire on dry, dead wood.

They remembered Eden.

The man and woman now lived in a world where death reigned, just as God had said. Their son Abel was gone. Their oldest son, Cain, was a murderer condemned to wander the earth alone. He was exiled from God's presence forever. To them, Cain too was dead.

Even they, since the day they ate, were dead—living dead.

Adam and Eve no longer had what they once had. The Lord God had been in them, joined to every fiber of their being. But now He was distant. His own Spirit-breathed life was no longer their empowering source of life. There was something else driving them from within. It was the deep, black, bottomless pit of need.

Of course, their real need was to return to the Lord. That was the answer. But, without their dynamic relationship with God, the fallen creatures were sentenced, like prisoners, to a lifetime of satisfying the endless needs of their self-centered desires.

Those needs were many, starting with food and water, clothing and shelter, survival and protection. But that bottomless pit demanded more and more. It required the ongoing gratification of sexual lust, the need to be recognized, to acquire more goods, to attain power, and be little gods reigning over others at will... The list went on and on.

But there was an option. For this broken world of sin, God provided His answer. If people would seek Him with all they had—heart, soul, mind, and strength—He would rescue them from the prison of their appetites. He would fill their insatiable needs with His infinite supply of love. It was His promise.

King David knew the wonder of that promise as he wrote:

The Lord is my shepherd, I shall not want... Even
though I walk through the valley of the shadow of
death, I fear no evil; for Thou art with me; Thy rod
and Thy staff, they comfort me (Ps. 23:1, 4).

David knew the secret of living in a fallen world: rely on God as the true provider of his life! With the Lord as his shepherd, the young sheep David would never lack anything. Even if he walked in death's shadow, the covenant promise stood firm: "Thou art with me." David chose to follow God and trust Him with his every need.

Jesus taught the same secret to His generation of anxious need seekers: "Seek first the kingdom of God and His righteousness; and all these things shall be added to you" (see Matt. 6:33). His answer was the same: God is the only supply of your appetites. Seek Him first.

But the Lord Jesus did not come just to teach us this lesson. He came to fulfill the deepest desire of our hearts: to reconcile us to His Father. He came to provide the way back to a living relationship with the Lord. How did He do this? By going the costly road to the cross. There could be no other way. Only there would the imprisoned human creature be perfectly set free, no longer held captive to this godless world, driven by selfish need.

By His death and resurrection, Jesus Christ opened the door to His Father, just as He said: "I am the way, and the truth, and the life; no one comes to the Father, but through me" (John 14:6). The Messiah had come. He had done his work. The invitation to return to the Eden kingdom, driven not by need but by God's love, was ours at last!

Provision in Christ

"Examine yourselves!" Paul penned. "Or do you not recognize this about yourselves, that Jesus Christ is in you?" (2 Cor. 13:5). Paul was tired of ministering to the constant needs of self-centered Christians. Didn't they know that the Lord of the universe was in them? By the Holy Spirit, they were born again and filled with God's life.

The time had come to address this issue of *need*:

Not that I speak from want; for I have learned to be content... in any and every circumstance I have learned the secret of being filled and going hungry, both of having abundance and suffering need. I can do all things through Him who strengthens me (Phil. 4:11-13).

Paul knew contentment. In any and every circumstance he depended on the daily power of Jesus Christ "who strengthens me." It *did not matter* whether all his earthbound, fleshly needs were met. At times he had abundance. At other times he went hungry and suffered need. At all times, Paul knew "the secret."

What is it? Need doesn't control our lives anymore! It's no longer lord and master over our lives. Believers have a new life source. We are in Christ, and Christ is in us. Like a steady ship on the storm-tossed sea of life's circumstances, the Lord Jesus is our answer. His daily power will strengthen us in every situation.

That's the secret of contentment. Not that Jesus will serve the god of our appetites. God forbid! But rather, we will serve the Lord Jesus only and trust our needs to His loving care.

Of course, Paul knew that some didn't understand this secret:

For many walk, of whom I often told you, and now tell you even weeping, that they are enemies of the

cross of Christ, whose end is destruction, whose god
is their appetite, and whose glory is in their shame,
who set their minds on earthly things (Phil. 3:18-19).

The empty bottomless pit of self-need—called appetite—
was the god of many so-called Christians. Of course, they
believed in Christ. But they believed in Him wrongly. They saw
Him as servant to their every desire, a genie granting wishes at
will.

They were enemies of the Cross of Christ. There is no way
to serve the god of appetite, driven by our sinful lusts for self-
satisfaction, and the Lord Jesus Christ. He demands true
repentance from our sins. This was their only hope, their only
way to avoid destruction. Then and only then would they know
the glory of God delivering them from the kingdom of need to
the kingdom of His love.

They were deceived, bit by the Eden serpent who has
always tried to arouse the appetites of believers, poisoned,
caught like Eve that day she felt desire and longed to satisfy her
new appetite in the name of God. It's how deception has worked
since Eden.

Paul wept for them, for he knew their end—destruction.

The Need Gospel

"He's here to meet your need tonight!" the preacher said. A
roar of applause went up. The congregation stood, clapping
their hands toward heaven, their faces displaying delight. "I
don't care what it is," he went on, "Lift it to Him. Believe what
the Word of God says: 'All things for which you pray and ask,
believe that you have received them, and they shall be granted
to you.'"

One woman fell into her seat crying. "No more!" she
thought to herself. She grabbed her winter-white coat, silk scarf,
Bible, and purse and bolted from the church. She had heard
enough.

Good for Food

Collette had once believed the preacher. Two years ago, she was close to a nervous breakdown. Her husband had dumped her for a younger woman, leaving her with three children and no skills or education to get a decent job. She thought life was over—that is, until a friend invited her to church. She was not much of a churchgoer. Religion wasn't her thing. But she went. What did she have to lose? It was a night out, something to do.

Something wonderful happened that night. Collette heard the saving news of Jesus Christ, and her heart was deeply moved. When the preacher gave an altar call after the sermon, she went forward and gave her life to the Lord Jesus, a new birth experience.

But now it was two years later. Collette had heard the same sermon week after week, like a broken record: "God is here to meet you at the point of your need. Just believe and have faith." She knew her need: She wanted a husband! She didn't want to raise her three sons alone, or work two jobs to meet the bills, or finish a long day all alone, in dead silence. Yes, Collette knew her need.

Yet God was not meeting her need. Why? What wasn't working? Was He angry with her? Didn't she have enough faith? But she had tried. She had prayed, believing the Lord would grant her request.

That cold winter night, she finally broke. She raced out of church because it hurt too much. Her life was in a shambles again. Her tears were more than the heartache of her loneliness. She had touched a deeper pain—she felt as if God was rejecting her.

"Wait!" a voice cried out behind her. She turned around and saw a priest running toward her. "I'm Fr. Lindsey," he said catching his breath. "I was visiting here tonight—I saw you leave."

As they walked the church grounds, she told him everything.

"You know, Collette," he said, "Jesus Christ has already met your greatest need. That's why He came. Look, our list of personal needs is endless. One day we're satisfied. The next we're not. But what does our heart really desire? It's Him, isn't it? And His promise is to be there. Just keep your eyes fixed on Christ."

He gently taught her the secret of contentment in Jesus. As he spoke, she felt the warmth of God's peace fill her heart.

Collette had heard the need gospel of old, one that concentrates on our appetites and begs God to meet them. When it works, we bless God. But when those needs are not met, we fall into despair, cursing God and finding our fulfillment somewhere else. It's a gospel that doesn't last.

We cannot accept this message, saying, "But it brings people to Christ." No, it does not. It leads to destruction. It snatches people from Christ. Though the Word enters their hearts, "the worries of the world, and the deceitfulness of riches, and the desires for other things enter in and choke the word..." (Mark 4:19).

The need gospel chokes the Word. It is a deceptive lie that promises God will meet our own, self-centered appetites. It feels good. It sounds scriptural, but it's not. It's the work of the Eden serpent arousing a seductive desire for the forbidden fruit.

And like Paul, we should weep.

Eight

DELIGHT TO THE EYES

"When the woman saw ... it was a delight to the eyes" (Gen. 3:6).

Eve was mesmerized. It was more than a need to satisfy her new hunger. She felt pleasure bubbling up inside her, like a geyser spouting skyward, overflowing in joy. Delight came simply from looking at the tree.

Eve had Christmas-morning eyes, like an innocent, wide-eyed and open-mouthed child seeing all her presents for the very first time. The thrill! The tree was hers. It had so much to offer.

As she touched the fruit, Eve concluded that the tree was more beautiful than anything she had yet seen in all of Eden. It radiated with a certain aura of mystery, suspense, as if, maybe, it had a thousand secrets to tell.

A thousand and more. The tree was a "delight to the eyes."

These feelings were strangely new to Eve, arousing pleasure and energizing her like never before, a sense-filled yearning. And they were strong, grabbing her attention with such force that God's words, "You shall surely die," no longer came to mind.

But the real sensation of delight went beyond what her physical eyes could see. The serpent had made a promise: Eating that fruit would open the door of her future. In her mind's eye, Eve saw herself seizing the promise and walking through that door.

In the twinkling of an eye, she could take, eat, and become all she had hoped to become in the Lord. She would be more like Him! Oh, what sheer ecstasy!

The serpent words were fresh, turning over and over in her mind. She had already made them her own: "My eyes will be opened. I will be like God. I will have the knowledge of good and evil"—all future-tense promises of what "will be" after she eats. No other tree offered that! No other tree made her feel this way.

Deception—it was all a mirage, a deceitful apparition. The serpent had created an illusion of beauty that appeared heaven-sent. Its magnetic appeal made Eve's visual senses come alive, enticing her to look, enticing her to dream, seducing her to sin.

Her physical eyes savored the moment. Her mind's eye looked into that godlike future. It was all there, right at her fingertips, just for her. Why wait? Eve felt a stirring passion to eat.

The Lust of the Eyes

The apostle John described the attraction Eve felt. He called it "the lust of the eyes" (1 John 2:16). It has always been Satan's job to create visual scenes that catch the believers' eyes and cause them to feel uncontrollable lust burning within them.

Delight to the Eyes

Those scenes appear in many different forms. For Eve it was a deceptive vision of a tree that could make her like God. For King David, the vision wasn't as godly, but Satan's goal was the same: to conceive lust, to make them *want* what their eyes see—an obsession strong enough to lead them away from the Lord.

That eye-lust captured David's heart.

He was known as the greatest warrior in all of Israel. As a young man, not yet twenty, David publicly fought and killed the mighty Philistine giant, Goliath. He became a national hero overnight. In every corner of Israel his praises rang out: "Saul has slain his thousands, and David his ten thousands" (1 Sam. 18:7).

Once made king, David drafted Israel's finest soldiers. His job was to conquer any foreign nation holding land in Israel. The objective was to force the enemy back, enlarge the borders, and capture the land that God had promised to Abraham's offspring.

Everywhere David went, God was with him. The battles were won, the army grew stronger, and the land was taken. The nation blossomed with economic prosperity. The Jews built up their towns, spread out their farms, and grew from a community of agricultural settlers into a flourishing empire. The blessings of God abounded.

It had all gone well for David—maybe too well.

One spring when war was mounting in the east, David decided to send the military out without him. He put someone else in command. He stayed home in Jerusalem. Perhaps he figured his men could handle the fight, or maybe he was tired. After all, David had won enough battles. He was nearing fifty. What challenge hadn't he faced?

It happened all too quickly. We don't know the exact details from Scripture. But perhaps the man of God, after lounging in bed most of the afternoon, took a walk on his palace roof. He saw the setting sun, a red-orange fireball, light the city with a breathtaking glow. The streets were bustling with people closing shop and farmers coming in from the fields—all heading home after a day's work—activity everywhere except inside David. As he watched the last piece of sun dip under the horizon, movement caught the corner of his eye.

Bathsheba.

From the roof he saw a woman bathing; and the woman was beautiful in appearance (see 2 Sam. 11:2).

David couldn't take his eyes off her. Such beauty! His heart began to race, pounding in his chest like a thunderous beating drum.

He felt alive again. The torch of life, seemingly blown out these past months, flared in passion. He thought he had lost it. But there it was inside him, revived just by looking at Bathsheba's lovely form.

He immediately dispatched his aids to find out more about this woman. When they came back, their report surprised him. What? Was this—Bathsheba? In that moment, he realized he knew her. She was the wife of his best friend, Uriah. She was the granddaughter of his closest confidant, Ahithophel. She was someone else's. Still, he couldn't take his eyes away—such delight.

The more he looked, the more he wanted.

The feeling gripped him—something stronger than sexual desire. If it was just that, David had a hundred wives at his call. But this was Bathsheba, a woman he could not rightfully have. His eyes danced. The time was right. She was alone, for Uriah was where David should have been—fighting in combat.

The gauntlet was thrown down. David had a challenge to face again. With his eyes still fixed on the woman, he whistled for a servant. The order was given: King David had sent for Bathsheba.

There was nothing deceptive about this moment. David was being tempted to sin. But in this case the devil's approach was the same as he used in Eden. He creates a lust of the eyes. For Eve, it was a deceptive, godly vision. For David, the sight was ungodly and he knew it. The lust of the eyes, a godly vision, an ungodly vision—it doesn't matter to Satan, as long as it leads God's own into sin.

The Vision of Power

The devil tried to create that eye-lust in Jesus:

> And he led Him up and showed Him all the kingdoms of the world in a moment of time. And the devil said to Him, "I will give You all this domain and its glory; for it has been handed over to me, and I give it to whomever I wish. Therefore, if You worship before me, it shall all be Yours" (Luke 4:5-7).

It was a miracle. Satan, parading his powers, led Jesus to a high spot and showed Him "in a moment of time ... all the kingdoms of the world ... and its glory"—a visual extravaganza, a show of shows!

Satan knew his work. He forced Jesus to see the kind of scenes only a king would long for—a tempting display, Satan hoped, that might do the trick and get Jesus on His knees.

It was not a mirage. The kingdoms had been "handed over" to Satan the second that Adam and Eve sinned. For, once exiled from Eden, they were condemned to live in the fallen world of darkness. This was Satan's dominion. He reigned as the "prince of the power of the air" (Eph. 2:2). It was his to give to whomever he wished.

The point was made. On the one hand, Jesus knew if He obeyed His Father's will, all the kingdoms would be His, and Satan would be crushed and dethroned. On the other hand, His Father's will would take Him down the hard road of suffering—the Cross road. There He would bear the weight of man's sin. There He would die all deaths for all time—and at what cost to His own soul?

The path to His ascension as Lord of lords was full of anguish and suffering. He who knew no sin would become sin. He who from eternity was united to His Father would endure separation from Him. He who deserved only God's perfect favor would enter into His Father's holy, consuming wrath against sin. This was the path to lordship.

Now Jesus could have it all for free. The kingdoms could be His now, this minute. Satan was offering Jesus immediate lordship in a moment of time. No suffering, no pain, no agonizing death on the cross. That's it. One yes from Jesus' mouth and a bow of His knee in adoration, and He could possess it all, cost-free.

There Jesus stood, His body weak from forty days and nights without food or water. The scene of glory magically played on and Satan waited, ready to close the deal. Just once more he whispered to God's Son, "I will give You all this domain and its glory."

The temptation. The lust of the eyes. And His answer: No.

This vision wasn't His Father's will. And what's more, it was a lie. This instant kingdom was not cost-free. It had a great cost. It required Jesus to worship Satan, and that He would not do. This time the old eye-pleasing, lust-breeding trick did not work.

The scene of glory disappeared the instant Jesus said no. With it the eye-tempting desire to have it vanished too. The same would have been true for Eve and for David had they said no.

In Sight of Glory

"Peter, come up here!" It was testimony time at church. The priest stepped back from the microphone as all eyes turned to see the great evangelist slowly, painfully, amble toward the podium.

He still had the famous Peter-smile and looked rather well,

having just gone through quadruple bypass surgery. But secretly I wished he had stayed seated. His testimonies are long and drawn out, preachy, and always about his favorite subject— himself.

I feared the worst. What was he going to say? Would he make light of his brush with death, act triumphant, and make us all wish we had his extraordinary faith? Or would he recognize his own human fears and testify, instead, of the greatness of our Lord Jesus Christ?

One thing was certain: His gospel didn't know heartache.

Peter was Mr. Always-Smiling Christian, who never had an off day. When he opened his mouth, there flowed a never-ending stream of testimonies jam-packed with Bible quotes. They all sounded the same. He was ministering in some far-off land with a well-known Christian leader, preaching to thousands of people ... and on and on.

He was a handsome, energetic man in his late sixties. From the day he accepted Christ, invitations to give his testimony poured in. He was a good ticket, a lovable one-man show. "Peter," people would tell him, "you're going to go places!"

He never promoted himself. They came to him in droves, ever painting a more glorious portrait of his career as an evangelist—traveling, a book, then maybe weekly radio shows and television.

"You will impact millions of people!" Peter saw the visions of splendor, brushed in colorful godly language, rolled out like a red carpet before him. They were wonderful scenes, all pointing to Christ and to the spreading of His gospel message worldwide.

And he bought it. His eyes saw nothing else.

"I had a heart attack six weeks ago," Peter said that Sunday morning with an uncharacteristic tremble in his voice. He told us how it happened: the ambulance ride, the doctors, the denial.

"You know, even as they wheeled me into that operating

room for open-heart surgery, I had victorious faith! I believed the Lord Jesus Christ would bless the operation with such great success that I'd be out preaching in less than a month's time. No problem.

"It wasn't until after the surgery, when I was half awake in the recovery room, that I heard the Holy Spirit speak to me. He said, 'Peter, repent of your sins and follow Me. Follow only Me.'

"What did He mean by that? I began to rehearse everything I had done for the Lord—every speaking engagement, the hundreds of people who had come forward at my meetings to receive Christ. I thought about my book, the people I knew, the spectacular miracles of healing.

"Then I heard Jesus' words from Scripture, 'Lord, Lord, did we not prophesy in Your name … and in Your name perform many miracles?'" Peter's voice broke. Real tears fell. His body shook. "And you know what Jesus told those people: 'I never knew you.'

"Didn't I know Him? Didn't I love Him? I knew the answer to those questions. For I knew what I loved. I loved the thrill of being known by the most famous Christian leaders of our time. And they liked me. They always sang my praises. That's what I loved.

"I thought I was doing it for Christ. I'm here to tell you that I have repented and asked His forgiveness. I'm here to ask you, will you help me? I want to follow Jesus Christ with all my heart and soul."

There wasn't a dry eye in the place that Sunday morning.

I was stunned by his testimony. This was a different man. What courage he had to make this confession. My own heart broke, for I always criticized Peter for his self-focus rather than praying for him and being his brother in Christ. I stayed away as the deceiver of old presented his godly visual presentation of glory. Peter saw it. He lusted for it and bought it. Just like the scene in the garden, the fame was nothing less than a delight to the eyes, a godlike delight.

Now he knew that vision wasn't God-sent. It was hell-sent. Thank God Peter heard the truth in the recovery room. The Spirit of Jesus had broken through the glitter of the serpent's spectacular show and offered him a chance to go free. And Peter said yes because he loved Jesus Christ more.

Nine

DESIRABLE TO MAKE ONE WISE

"When the woman saw ... that the tree was desirable
to make one wise, she took from its fruit and ate"
(Gen. 3:6).

A new Eden was at hand. As Eve plucked the knowledge
fruit from the tree, she knew something greater,
something more perfect was about to break into her life.
Like a foaming white ocean wave ready to crash on the shore, a
new world was seconds away.

She took the fruit with sincerity. There were no dark, evil
motives lurking around inside her. She was made in the image
and likeness of God, sinless and without evil. Her innocence
believed the serpent. Her pure childlike trust welcomed him as
a friend and fellow lover of God.

But the serpent pounced on her naïveté. In the name of God,
he guaranteed that the knowledge of good and evil would better

her relationship with the Lord. She would know, like God knows.

Eve didn't have that knowledge yet. If she had missed something in her walk with God, she wanted it! She wanted to please Him. She wanted to be in His will. More than anything, she wanted to know the Lord fully, with His knowledge and perfect wisdom.

How odd to imagine the perfect, sinless woman of God could feel something missing, an emptiness. In truth, there was nothing lacking. But the professional salesman serpent had changed all that. He made her think she was less than perfect. She needed something more, something that would make her more like God. The salesman's work was bold, daring: He convinced her she did have an emptiness within, a deep longing need (even though she didn't), and then he offered the means for her to satisfy the need.

One taste and that wisdom was hers. As she held the knowledge fruit in the palm of her hand, she felt that empty vacuum of space inside her: It was "desirable to make one wise." The deeper knowledge of God—what longing, what aching desire to possess the riches of His wisdom! And she believed the friendly serpent.

I understand Eve. Her serpent was like my stranger, the one I never met because I was warned, "Don't talk to strangers!"

They told me the stranger would act like a friend. He would know me by name and offer me the kind of candies that make little boys jump up and down! Yes, good for food. He'd show me toys and let me ride in the front seat of his sports car, delighting my eyes.

But more, even much more—he would have a special knowledge about my parents, a knowledge I would not have. What was it? Maybe my mom had something come up—a sudden change in plans. Before she left, she asked this friendly man to pick me up from school.

To believe the stranger is to follow the stranger. One step into the front seat of his race car, with sweets and toys galore, and I'd be obeying my mother. That's what the stranger said, and he "knew" firsthand. Now I know what Mom wants, so I get in—just as with Eve and her friend.

A new life in the deeper knowledge of God awaited Eve. Just one bite and a more glorious paradise, with God's smiling nod of approval, was all hers. She would truly "know" the Lord.

Filled with a godly desire to be wise, Eve believed she was doing the Lord's will. She was sincere—but sincerely wrong. As she put the fruit to her lips, her teeth sank quickly into the meat, and her expectations soared with hope in God. Oh, how she believed.

Just then, Eve stepped into a new Eden.

Danger to the Unsuspecting

Paul, like Eve, desired with a pure heart to know the Lord. Nothing else mattered to him: "I count all things to be loss in view of the surpassing value of knowing Christ Jesus my Lord" (Phil. 3:8). In his sold-out love for Jesus, Paul knew one thing.

He knew the warning. He had learned the lesson of Paradise: deceivers prey on the pure in heart, the innocent and blameless. Paul preached this Eden message to the young churches so that, in their undivided love for the Lord Jesus, they might remember Eve (see 2 Cor. 11:3).

So did Moses. He cautioned the Israelites when he told them false prophets would arise, performing miraculous signs and wonders. Even so, he warned, they were not to follow them, no matter what.

> You shall not listen to the words of that prophet or that dreamer of dreams ... because he has counseled rebellion against the Lord your God ... to seduce you from the way in which the Lord your God commanded you to walk (Deut. 13:3-5).

The key word is *seduce*. The false prophets tried to seductively lure believers away from the path God commanded them to walk. Moses knew the Genesis 3 story and warned his own generation.

The writer of Proverbs flagged the same deception. In poetic language, the writer turned God's wisdom into a woman who had built her house, set her table, and went to the middle of town to evangelize the naive. She wanted them to know the way of God:

> She calls from the tops of the heights of the city: "Whoever is naive, let him turn in here!" To him who lacks understanding she says, "Come, eat of my food and drink of the wine I have mixed. Forsake your folly and live, and proceed in the way of understanding" (Prov. 9:3-6).

But there was another woman—the woman of folly. She was an identical twin to the woman portraying God's wisdom. She too built her house, set her table, and went to the middle of the town evangelizing:

> Calling to those who pass by, who are making their paths straight: "Whoever is naive, let him turn in here."
> And to him who lacks understanding she says, "Stolen water is sweet; and bread eaten in secret is pleasant."
> But he does not know that the dead are there, that her guests are in the depths of Sheol (Prov. 9:15-18).

The woman of folly sounded like the wisdom woman. But she wasn't. She was a deceiver. The naive entered her house, ate her meal, and thought they were keeping their paths straight. They did not know they were in the depths of Sheol, dining with the dead.

Two voices cried out the same words: "Whoever is naive, let him turn in here!" The one, the voice of the seductress, did not have God's wisdom, which demanded that the naive forsake their folly and live. Like the garden serpent, the woman of folly sold a look-alike wisdom (the knowledge of good and evil) that led to death.

In the end, it's not enough for someone to want to know the Lord. Those seeking after God must discern the truth. They cannot remain naive, for there are two voices, sounding the same, calling out for their souls. One is true wisdom. One is serpent wisdom.

There must be discernment. John put it this way:

> These things I have written to you concerning those who are trying to deceive you … Beloved, do not believe every spirit, but test the spirits to see whether they are from God; because many false prophets have gone out into the world (1 John 2:26, 4:1).

John wrote warning Christians not to believe just anyone. Why did he do that? He knew Satan was at work in the churches "trying to deceive." For this reason, he urged them to put to the test those who professed to have the Lord's wisdom, to see "whether they are from God."

Jesus put this truth into practice. He tested the religious leaders of His day. When He was done, He knew the voice of folly:

> Woe to you, scribes and Pharisees, hypocrites, because you travel about on sea and land to make one proselyte [convert]; and when he becomes one, you make him twice as much a son of hell as yourselves (Matt. 23:15).

The test was over: The Pharisees had failed. They had built their houses, set their tables, and traveled the world over trying to win one convert. Instead of winning souls for the Lord, they plundered the naive. When all was done, their convert was "twice as much a son of hell" as themselves.

Our Lord and Savior Jesus Christ reinforced the principles of Genesis 3: Sincerity is not enough. It must be coupled with a discernment that tests. Otherwise, the naive will blindly follow the serpent's seductive knowledge, and that is deadly. Sincerity without discernment is always deadly. It is the lesson from the garden.

The apostles and prophets received instruction from Genesis 3. As often as they preached the good news of life-changing relationship with the Lord, they recalled Eve's encounter with the serpent. They warned the pure in heart, the innocent and naive so that, if possible, they might save them from Satan's folly, for they knew the voice of God's wisdom is never heard alone.

A seductive sound-alike voice is also heard—one that captures "the hearts of the unsuspecting" (Rom. 16:18). In every generation, this voice of folly is heard. Ours is no different. It's our job to proclaim danger to the unsuspecting, lest they follow the other wisdom, the other woman, and learn when it is too late: Her guests are in the depths of Sheol dining with the dead.

The Knowledge That Puffs Up

I was chaplain on duty the night Kevin was brought into the hospital. The ambulance had radioed ahead: Code Red. The emergency code team flew into place to help another victim of a drunk driver.

When the stretcher came in, I caught a momentary glimpse of his crushed body. The ambulance workers were shouting enough medical lingo to tell me that Kevin, twenty-six, was already near death.

I knew Kevin. His family had been in our church for years. I called his parents at once. They rushed to the hospital, only to wait as the long hours passed by slowly. When the doctor finally came out, he gave no hope. It was, in his opinion, only a question of time. The doctor's last words faded—"I'm sorry."

Kevin lived the night ... and the week.

I got to the hospital in the early mornings and late afternoons. Nearly every morning at half past six, a group of Christians flocked around Kevin's bed. As I watched from outside the room, I could hear them reciting passages from Scripture about healing.

Then, at the end of each reading, the words, "We claim your healing in the name of Jesus," were said over his motionless body.

On the fourth day, the pastor came out of the room and made a beeline for me. He flashed his Bible and walked with a glowing confidence. He spoke, knowing I was Kevin's minister.

"Kevin has regained consciousness," he began, with a certain sound of victory in his voice. He seemed to have the kind of faith that could move mountains. "We praise God for that. It's a triumph over Satan because God has told us Kevin is going to be healed. We are fighting against the strongholds of Satan for this brother's life. And Jesus will have the victory." He did not wait for my response. He patted me on the shoulder almost patronizingly, and sped off down the hospital corridor.

I was flooded with questions as I watched this man walk away with an air of authority. Why did he seem so arrogant? Or was this a real confidence that God had truly spoken about Kevin's healing? I wondered what he would say if I asked him, What happens if you have heard wrongly? Do we not test prophecies? What if this one fails—what will you tell your followers? Doesn't that put the focus of everyone on the promise of healing rather than on the Lord Himself? Isn't that dangerous? If the Lord has spoken, then let Him confirm that word!

One thing was true. Kevin had regained consciousness in the night. But when I went to see him, he told me quite a different story.

"I'm going to die," Kevin confided to me. A tender smile lit his face. "I had a dream last night. Jesus came to my bedside and said, 'Kevin, I am coming to take you home so you can be with Me forever.' His hand touched me, and I felt this—incredible peace. I can't explain it. I just knew everything was going to be okay. He's coming for me. And I want to be with Him."

He looked up at me and, as if he wanted to convince me,

said, "I don't want to live in this broken body." I felt the strength of his hand, saw the light shining in his eyes, heard the gentle timbre of his voice, and I knew Kevin's peace. It seemed as though this young man was headed home.

He lived three more days.

I went to the hospital the morning after Kevin died. I got there to see the pastor and his crew leaving the room with shock on their faces, the bed empty and Kevin gone. I walked over to the pastor. I thought he might want to know Kevin's dream. I hoped it might comfort him and shed a certain light on the young man's relationship with the Lord. I got no more than five words out when the pastor put up his hand and stopped me.

"God wanted him healed!" It felt like he was speaking more to his followers than to me. "God came to me personally and told me he would live if we fought against Satan. Now Kevin is dead. Dead!

"Brother," he preached at me, "you need the kind of faith that heals the sick. Jesus could not heal in Nazareth because of unbelief. We are praying for you, Pastor. Let me ask you, have you received the Lord as your personal Savior?"

He turned, his followers at his side, and walked away.

It felt like a knife piercing my soul. Was he blaming me— my lack of faith— for Kevin's death? Was he blaming the devil? Why did I now feel like an unrepentant sinner who did not know the Lord? Where was the love of God? Why did the stench of arrogance fill my nostrils with the sense that this pastor, and he alone, held the key to God's knowledge?

"Knowledge," Paul wrote to the Corinthians, "makes arrogant [puffs up], but love edifies" (1 Cor. 8:1). If only the pastor had put aside his arrogance, he would have been able to listen to Kevin's testimony. For the Lord *had* spoken. He had come to Kevin by night with His peace that surpasses understanding in His right hand and His grace to exit this world in His left. The Lord Jesus Christ of heaven and earth had given Kevin the homeward-bound ticket to paradise.

But this pastor could not hear the voice of God's wisdom speaking to Kevin in this situation. He had listened to the Lord in prayer—but he did not want to put what he heard to the test. For even in Kevin's death, he refused to see that his own position had failed him. Even then, he could not see that he had heard wrongly. Now was the time to wrestle with his faith. But instead, he strengthened himself, defended his stand, and put the blame into the court of the devil and me.

The pastor did not test his prophecy. Therefore, he listened to the other voice. He bought it, he became puffed up, and in the name of the Lord, he led his followers—the naive—down the same path.

"Beloved, do not believe every spirit, but test the spirits to see whether they are from God; because many false prophets have gone out into the world" (1 John 4:1).

Ten

TEMPTATION

"She gave also to her husband with her, and he ate"
(Gen. 3:6).

The deception was over. The soured taste of forbidden fruit lingered in her mouth. Her hands still clutched the weapon. This was not a new Eden. Eve had plunged into some other world. She could touch the evil inside her—formless, void, and dark.

She instantly knew, with a shock bolting through her body: The serpent had lied. He wasn't God's friend, and the tree was not the path to a deeper relationship with the Lord. The tree, just like God had said, was the death tree. And she had eaten from it.

Eve had disobeyed. In her pursuit of the Lord, she had been deceived. But was it her choice? How could it be? She was tricked, just like the deer that eats the bait, having no idea that the hunter's trap springs with just one bite. In deception, Eve did not choose between good and evil. She chose between perfection and greater perfection, glory and greater glory. No, she did not willingly choose to sin. Of course not. The crafty serpent was to blame. As she turned to him, her blood boiling, it was too late. He was long gone. He had left her alone to feel the torture, her soul stripped from Eden's glory—raped and shattered.

But the serpent's work had only begun. His master plan was just half-finished. He wanted the couple—and Adam hadn't eaten yet.

The man never saw the serpent. He only saw Eve, the forbidden fruit lodged in her hands, partly eaten, and that face. Something had changed, for the moment he looked at her, she blushed.

Her hands moved quickly to cover her nakedness. She slipped behind the knowledge tree, filled with embarrassment. She knew she was naked, and she couldn't stand the thought of Adam seeing her.

As he came toward her, their eyes locked together. The man and his wife were in two separate worlds, and they both knew it. Eve lifted her hands to him, the fruit held in suspension between their worlds. There were no words. As Adam touched her hands, she gave him the forbidden fruit and backed away, behind the tree.

She wanted him to eat. She didn't want to stay in the kingdom of good and evil alone. Eve needed him, not in his God-made perfection, but as she was, exiled in her soul from paradise.

There were no words.

This was not deception. Adam was faced with a real choice: to obey God or to follow his wife into disobedience. There were no serpents in disguise, no false promises, no deluded visions of grandeur. Unlike Eve, he knew this was a decision between life and death.

In truth, there was a world war raging inside him. He faced the enemy of his soul, and it was not the devil. It was his fallen wife. His love for God and his love for Eve were fighting against each other, each demanding he choose, forcing him to decide.

Would he step back and call on the Lord to come to his rescue? Or would he take the fruit, now lying loosely in the palm of his hand, and join his wife in the world of evil and death?

He was man in God's image, holding the right to choose.

And he ate.

Deception or Temptation?

Both Adam and Eve ate. In that action, both sinned against God. But Scripture highlights the difference in how they fell from the grace of God: "And it was not Adam who was deceived, but the woman being quite deceived, fell into transgression" (1 Tim. 2:14).

Eve was "quite deceived." Satan had come dressed as an Eden friend—and tricked her into believing the godless fruit was a godly choice. She was blameless, duped by the deceiver into sin.

But Adam was not deceived.

He was tempted. Satan's kingdom appeared to him in the person of fallen Eve, tempting him to disobey the commandment. Adam faced a knowing decision. He was fully aware that Eve's once-eaten fruit led to the kingdom of death, an act of rebellion against his Lord.

For this reason, the New Testament identifies the entrance of sin through the man Adam: "Therefore, just as through one man sin entered the world, and death through sin, and so death spread to all men, because all sinned" ... (Rom. 5:12). For Adam, not Eve, exercised his free will in full knowledge of what he was doing. He knew his decision was between God and

Eve, obedience and disobedience, heaven and hell. So Scripture identifies Adam as the one who brought sin and death into the world—original sin—by the action of his choice.

Temptation is a clear choice. Unlike deception, the temptation to sin is never disguised: "Be of sober spirit, be on the alert. Your adversary, the devil, prowls about like a roaring lion, seeking someone to devour. But resist him, firm in your faith" (1 Pet. 5:8-9).

Christians are called to be on the alert when the devil's unmasked—a prowling, devouring adversary who must be resisted.

When Jesus endured His temptation in the wilderness, He met face-to-face with the tempter (see Matt. 4:3). The devil came dressed as himself, the angel of darkness, hoping to lure Jesus into sin.

Paul also knew the danger of temptation. In one of his earliest writings, he penned his own fears. He was afraid the church at Thessalonica had knowingly fallen to the magical charms of the tempter:

> When I could endure it no longer, I also sent to find
> out about your faith, for fear that the tempter might
> have tempted you, and our labor should be in vain
> (1 Thess. 3:5).

As often as Paul taught on deception, he also taught the faithful about Satan the tempter. He warned the church not to embrace his temptations but rather "to stand firm against the schemes of the devil" lest their faith should be in vain (Eph. 6:11).

What is temptation? It's a knowing awareness that sin is at hand, crouching at our door, inviting us to choose against God.

Like Adam, we find ourselves at the crossroad, deciding between God's path and sin's path. It is a clear choice. James put it this way: "Therefore, to one who knows the right thing to do, and does not do it, to him it is sin" (James 4:17).

For example, a Christian businessman in Virginia was caught pilfering money from his company. When his boss found out, he was fired. He later told his minister: "Creditors were threatening my family night and day. I was desperate for cash—desperate enough to steal the money. It was wrong. I knew as I was doing it I was sinning against my Lord."

The Christian who is tempted by sin knows the right thing to do. The red warning signal of the Holy Spirit flashes in that person's heart saying, "Don't sin. Make the choice to follow Me."

The choice may be hard, the temptation appealing.

> But each one is tempted when he is carried away and enticed by his own lust. Then when lust has conceived, it gives birth to sin; and when sin is accomplished, it brings forth death (James 1:14-15).

James described the birth cycle of temptation. First, we are enticed by sin. Second, if we choose to entertain the sin, lust is conceived. Third, we play with it in our mind, pondering it over time until it has gone full term (like any pregnancy). Then, at last, lust gives birth to sin, and sin brings forth death.

At any point before committing the sin, we have the choice to abort the temptation. It's as real a choice as Adam possessed in the garden. It's a knowing choice—black and white—that is always given when Satan comes as tempter. But watch out! It's a choice never given when he comes as deceiver.

Knowing the Right Thing to Do

The board of elders' meeting ended in a dispute—again.

Tony, the senior pastor, in his grand preaching style, gave an upbeat closing message. It denied any hint of the tension that packed the room tight. It encouraged some people, but it angered more.

Of course, no one knew the reason for the dispute—not that night, anyway. The church business was in order. Attendance was up, and so were the finances. Positive reports came in from the various church ministries. There were no hot issues on the table. But there was tension.

It felt like a dark thundercloud oppressively hanging over the church. Those who had eyes to see knew that division was ripping relationships apart: brother against brother, family against family. The peace of the Lord Jesus Christ was being driven away.

The problem was Steve, the assistant pastor.

Many in the congregation were blinded by Steve's quiet magnetism. His godly presence was inviting, gentle like a dove, rich in comfort. His soft green eyes and warm, genuine smile made the stranger feel welcomed, as though they had found a long-lost friend.

Steve had a way of loving and needing love that flocked the needy to his side. He had a loyal following in the church. They loved him so deeply that, when criticism came against Steve, they rigorously defended him to the end, even beyond common reason.

And there were criticisms. About a year after he arrived at the church, rumors cropped up charging Steve with an addiction to both alcohol and sexual misconduct. There were even stories that he was soliciting personal contributions from his followers.

Pastor Tony ended the rumors.

"I want to hear nothing more about Steve," he told the board of elders. "I receive testimonies every week from people touched by his ministry. They feel this church has been blessed by God to have him here. And so do I. Because of Steve, our Sunday services are filled. We're turning people away. Has that happened before?

"These testimonies," he concluded, "should tell you we're in the center of God's perfect will. I hope I've made myself clear."

Tony had made the decision to stick by Steve. No one could

convince him—though many tried—that a dividing schism was slowly, methodically, killing the church like a cancerous growth.

Pastor Steve was there four years before the cancer erupted with its fatal wound. His wife suddenly appeared at the September elders' meeting, her face swollen and her body badly bruised.

"Someone has to stop Steve," she cried. She testified of the drinking, the physical abuse, and his many sexual outings with young, needy women. The secret was out—Steve's deceptions exposed.

Steve, dressed as the trusting, caring pastor, had perfected the outward Christian image. He was a deceiver who used his position to satisfy his own unresolved problems. Now, finally, it was over. No one else would fall victim to his disguised disease.

Though many were deceived, one was not—Pastor Tony.

When the rumors first came to his attention early on, Tony confronted Steve. With a seemingly repentant heart, Steve made an open confession and a sincere promise to seek professional help.

Tony knew everything: the addiction to alcohol and sex, the tendency to attract and abuse the needy, the physical beatings of his wife. He also knew Steve never fulfilled his promise to seek professional help. Tony knew the story. He faced a clear choice.

Either he could have stopped Steve by reporting his conduct to the local bishop. Or he could say nothing, quiet the church elders, and act as if nothing ever happened—sweep it under the rug.

The temptation to sin was real for Tony. All of his prayers longed for a successful church. And here it was! Steve's charisma played a big part in that success. They were a good team together; and if he left, Tony feared it all might come crashing down.

"What would happen," he thought, "if I fired Steve?

Everyone would know that he was the reason for the success of this church. I have failed for so many years. And now, it's everything I have ever dreamed of. I can't do it. I can't let him go. I need him."

Tony, like Adam, met the tempter, held the fruit in his hand, and ate.

The Door of Opportunity

Jesus gave His disciples authority in the Holy Spirit: "Behold, I have given you authority to tread upon serpents and scorpions, and over all the power of the enemy, and nothing shall injure you" (Luke 10:19). There was provision to withstand the enemy.

The early church taught believers how to stand in that authority. If Satan came armed with his temptations, Christians were not to fear: "Resist the devil and he will flee from you" (James 4:7). It was that simple. Satan cannot injure the church resting in the death and resurrection of the Lord Jesus Christ— cannot.

The Scriptures have never wavered on this point. Since the day Adam sinned, a knowing act of rebellion toward God, believers have been taught to say no to temptation in the Spirit's power.

The problem comes when we do not resist.

Paul sounded the warning: "And do not give the devil an opportunity" (Eph. 4:27). When temptations come, the decision to resist must be made. If not, that dark door of opportunity opens.

For some Christians, confrontation is scary. It's easier to take a passive approach: "It wasn't me who invited the temptation here. Satan barged in. I'm not responsible!" It is even easier to turn away and pretend the tempter never passed through the door.

Yet, any time we allow the unmasked, devouring adversary

opportunity, we make a choice. It is the choice that says yes to temptation. It's also the decision *not* to stand in the authority of the Holy Spirit given us by the Lord Jesus Christ—a clear choice.

We must have the courage to stand in that authority and say "No!" For the statement is true and worthy of our God—if we cannot actively resist Satan the tempter, the known enemy, how shall we actively confront Satan the deceiver, the disguised enemy?

Our fundamental decision must remain firm when Satan comes as the tempter: Do not give the devil an opportunity. It is this resolve, sure and steadfast, that will strengthen our awareness of being alert to Satan when he comes as the deceiver, dressed as an angel of light.

Part III

THE ANGUISH

Eleven

DIVISION FROM EACH OTHER

"Then the eyes of both of them were opened, and they knew that they were naked; and they sewed fig leaves together and made themselves loin coverings" (Gen. 3:7).

Adam and Eve were together again. The twice-eaten fruit dropped from Adam's hand and rolled under the forbidden tree, discarded waste littering God's perfect creation. It, like Adam and Eve, no longer belonged in Paradise.

Adam was a stranger in his own home. Standing in the bright God-light of Eden, he knew he had plummeted into an ungodly dark and terrible death kingdom. He felt the torture of being in hell but living in glory. Sinless Adam knew full immersion into sin.

Adam and Eve were together in sin, joined in their mutual eating of the forbidden fruit and their ensuing fall into Satan's kingdom.

Their eyes were opened. As someone who is born again sees and enters the kingdom of God (see John 3:3-5), so Adam and Eve were, if you will, born again into the "domain of darkness" (Col. 1:13). They could not see this kingdom before they sinned. But now, their eyes were opened. They both saw and entered the godless world of evil.

And they were naked. Adam, like a frightened animal, darted away the moment Eve peered out from behind her tree. She saw him! She saw his naked body and that was embarrassing. Adam took cover behind a neighboring fig tree and felt his own face blush red.

They were hiding from each other, ashamed to expose their nakedness. Eve behind the God-forbidden tree, Adam behind the fig tree—this had never happened before. Since their creation they had walked in Eden "naked and ... not ashamed" (Gen. 2:25). But not anymore. The couple, under bush covering, felt shame.

They were separated. Sin had done its work. The love of God they once shared, love that made their hearts one, was gone.

As their eyes met from behind their respective trees, Adam and Eve experienced their first "knowledge" of evil: sin divides. A great and terrible chasm stood between them. Their love for each other, rooted in God's love, had been violently rent asunder. Sin had ripped their souls into two.

What were they to do? They decided to make loin coverings by sewing fig leaves together. These garments would hide their nakedness and allow them to come out of hiding, without shame. It worked! Adam and Eve stepped away from the trees—dressed.

But it didn't work. Fig leaves could never solve their real problem—they were in sin. And where there is sin, there is division. It's the mark of the fallen kingdom. For even though they could stand together again, Adam and Eve were still a separated people living in a kingdom of division—still two hearts, feeling their souls alone, without the other.

Korah: The Rumblings of Division

A blasting trumpet sound in the middle of the night meant one thing to a sleeping Israelite in the Old Testament: "Wake up! Move! The enemy is advancing toward the city." War was at hand.

But the trumpet never sounded when the enemy was inside the city, disguised like a serpent deceiver. The watchmen kept their eyes fixed on the horizon. It wasn't their job to spot deceivers.

But there was a warning, a kind of trumpet blast, for those who had ears to hear. It was the sound of division stirring among the people. As a doctor knows that fever is a sign of infection, so the Lord's prophets knew that division from within was a sign of the deceiver at work.

It's a true and trustworthy statement: To see the deceiver is to find division, and to see division is to find the deceiver.

Moses experienced this truth. It wasn't the silver trumpets blowing the battle cry (see Num. 10:1-10) that warned him of the enemy. Not this time. It was a new sound, one that announced the enemy was a deceiver inside the camp, an opponent most dangerous. That sound?

The rumbling of division. It was Korah, a Levitical priest. He rose up against Moses and Aaron in the sight of all Israel:

> You have gone far enough, for all the congregation
> are holy, every one of them, and the Lord is in their
> midst; so why do you exalt yourselves above the
> assembly of the Lord? (Num. 16:3).

Korah had ambition. He wanted a shot at being high priest someday like Aaron. He was sick of Moses and Aaron's leadership and their exalted positions. In his opinion, it was time they step down.

Of course, Korah was a politician. He had carefully planned his move to power. Over time he had gathered a commanding and influential following: "two hundred and fifty leaders of the congregation, chosen in the assembly, men of renown" (Num. 16:2).

Korah had engineered a power play with two hundred fifty leaders and over fourteen thousand Israelites (see Num. 16:49). Although the Hebrews numbered in the area of two million, Korah had the strength to make his move. His followers stood at his side when he spoke to Moses and Aaron.

Moses knew he faced the inside enemy. He also knew that Korah's sin was more than selfish ambition grumbling after Aaron's job. This was a heart sinning against the Lord. Moses responded:

> You have gone far enough, you sons of Levi!
> Therefore you and all your company are gathered
> together against the Lord; but as for Aaron, who is he
> that you grumble against him? (Num. 16:7, 11).

Moses never defended his leadership. The next day, with the entire nation gathered together at the tabernacle, the "glory of the Lord appeared" with judgment in His right hand (Num. 16:19).

Moses uttered the sentence of God: "These men have spurned the Lord." With that, Korah and the two hundred fifty leaders were swallowed "alive into Sheol" (see Num. 16:30-33). The division was over. The Lord had rescued Israel from its war against the deceiver enemy.

The New Testament writer Jude labeled Korah a deceiver (see Jude 11-13). For even though Korah was a leader and a priest of the Lord who served daily in the ministry of God's holy worship, he was a man who caused "divisions" (Jude 19). He was a man of deception.

The rebellion of Korah would stand as a memorial forever: When the serpent deceiver is at work, division is sure to follow.

Jude made his point: Korah's example wouldn't be forgotten.

No Division in the Body

"But if you bite and devour one another," Paul wrote to the Galatians, "take care lest you be consumed by one another" (Gal. 5:15). Division had run through the Galatian churches like a dry summer brushfire. It was devouring and consuming believers.

"You were running well," he went on. "Who hindered you from obeying the truth?" (Gal. 5:7). Paul wanted to know who was behind the division. He knew the telltale sign of the deceiver.

His words cut sharp like a knife, as if he faced Satan himself: "Would that those who are troubling you would even mutilate themselves" (Gal. 5:12). He wanted the fiery division stopped.

Paul never found it hard to spot the serpent. He understood the church to be more than a crowd of believers, each having a personal relationship with the Lord Jesus Christ. A Christian was someone joined to the living community called the body of Christ.

He once wrote, "By one Spirit we were all baptized into one body" (1 Cor. 12:13). That is the church! In baptism, the Holy Spirit forever unites Christian with Christian. Though the church is made up of many believers, the Scriptures call it "one body."

Christians, therefore, cannot be out on their own. They are a together people joined in God the Holy Spirit to one another, a loving church of believers. In the same way, Christians cannot divide from each other. When they do, the whole community knows it. And everyone suffers because of it. Therefore, the statement is forever true: With Jesus our Lord as head of the church, His body, "there should be no division in the body" (1 Cor. 12:25).

No division: The apostles constantly warned against any uprisings in the churches. They required the elders to stay alert, spot the divisions, and arrest the deceivers behind the trouble.

For example, Paul wrote these words to the Roman elders:
Now I urge you, brethren, keep your eye on those
who cause dissensions and hindrances contrary to the
teaching which you learned, and turn away from
them. For ... they deceive the hearts of the
unsuspecting (Rom. 16:17-18).

It is a simple rule found in the Scriptures, known since the
days of Eden: Deceivers cause dissension. The elders in Rome
were urged to keep their eyes on them and to turn away from
them.

The apostle Paul always exhorted the churches to diligently
"preserve the unity of the Spirit in the bond of peace" (Eph. 4:3).
As long as that Spirit-unity was maintained, under the headship
of Jesus Christ, the deceiver enemy didn't have a chance.

His only chance came when believers lost the unity of the
Holy Spirit. Then the devil would put on his disguise and make
his move. He'd spread the wildfire of division through the
church, hindering believers from obeying the truth. It's the way
the serpent of old has always worked—inside the camp.

Uprising in the Church

It was an ice-cold Sunday morning in mid-January. The
night sky hadn't yet seen the sun when Rick pulled into the
church parking lot. He always spent an hour in his office alone
before the services. Everyone knew about that hour. It was
never violated.

He opened the door and—surprise! The lights were on and
the place was packed with people, all familiar faces. Some
people were standing, some sitting. Walter and Sarah stood out.
He felt their eyes boring into him. Rick could feel the anger in
the air.

"Good morning, everyone," Rick said politely. His eyes
slowly moved around the room to each person. "What can I do
for you?"

"We want changes," Walter spoke out.

"Why now? Why a meeting before a Sunday worship?"

"How else can we get your attention?" Walter came back. His heavy-set face turned a tomato red. "We have tried to talk to you, but you won't listen. Maybe now you'll know we mean business!"

"We're really not happy," Dolores said under her breath. The word *we* caught Rick. He wondered how long they had been a *we*.

"Before you came," she went on, "this church was on fire for Jesus. We had an altar call every Sunday morning. Our worship was free, and we were bringing people into a closer walk with Christ."

"It's becoming too damn traditional," Fred interrupted. "All the old folks, who have been here since God knows when, they're the ones taking over this church. You're forcing us out."

"It's that simple, Rick," Walter stated boldly. "We're asking for changes around here. We don't want organ music at Sunday services, or fall bazaars, or women's groups to dress the altar. You know what that is? It's the devilish traditional snares creeping back into this church. We want to get back to the pure gospel!

"We want the old-time evangelistic sermons with altar calls at the end. Turn this church on fire with the Holy Spirit, Rick!" Walter came up to him and placed his hand on Rick's shoulder: "We know you can do it. Plus, let's be honest. Those old folks don't even know Jesus as their Savior and Lord!"

One man yelled, "Right!"

There was a sudden turnaround. This group was now on Rick's side, as if he was their candidate to make the necessary changes. The whole room was now filled with hope: "Come on, Rick! You're a Spirit-filled pastor who preaches Jesus Christ. You can do it!"

Rick looked into Walter's eyes without expression, face-to-face. "And if I don't meet your demands, then what happens?"

The mood changed again. A deafening hush fell on the room.

"Then we leave. We start a church of our own. My wife and I have offered our home as a place to start. We will do it, Rick. We don't want to—this is our home church—but we will."

Division. And it sounded so godly, so righteous.

The meeting ended abruptly. It was time for the service. As the room emptied, Rick's mind filled with their lingering words: "We want changes ... Those old folks don't know Jesus ... devilish traditional snares ... You can do it ... We'll start a church of our own."

Rick went to his desk and pushed his sermon notes aside. Rick had never faced rebellion in Jesus' name before. But there it was: the stench of division in the body of Christ, all cloaked in God-talk. Rick knew this was just like Korah, just like the divisions Satan always brings to the people of God, disguised and deadly.

"Holy Spirit," he prayed, "stop the uprising in our midst."

Rick left the office without his sermon notes. The time had come to preach on the deceiver—and his rumblings of division.

Twelve

DIVISION FROM GOD

The couple had come out of hiding, garbed in fig leaves. Eve had just begun to tell Adam the story of the serpent and how she thought she was going to be like God, when ... *that* sound.

They both stopped in dead silence. That sound was the first sound they had ever heard and loved. It used to make their hearts leap with joy like a dancer soaring through the air! But not now. This was different. For an instant, they stood frozen in fear:

> And they heard the sound of the Lord God walking in the garden in the cool of the day, and the man and his wife hid themselves from the presence of the Lord God among the trees of the garden (Gen. 3:8).

It was Him, and He was coming closer. His immediate presence filled Eden with even more glory than the garden possessed. Within seconds before His arrival, that presence touched Adam and Eve, driving them away, back under cover, behind their trees.

This time, the fig leaves didn't work.

They felt the Lord's presence pierce beyond their clothing. It penetrated into their hearts, making them feel naked and ashamed all over again. And, like before, their reaction was to hide. By the time the Lord came on the scene, the couple was gone. Only the half-eaten forbidden fruit remained in the open, dead still.

Once again, Adam and Eve were hiding, and hiding means separation. But this time it was not from each other. It was from God.

> Then the Lord God called to the man, and said to
> him, "Where are you?" And he said, "I heard the
> sound of Thee in the garden, and I was afraid
> because I was naked; so I hid myself" (Gen. 3:9-10).

The Lord God spoke to "the man." That seemed right. After all, it was Adam who *knowingly* made the free choice to sin against Him.

He started with a question: "Where are you?" The Lord often asks questions in Scripture. Obviously He knows the answers. He's God! He asks them for our sake, that we might articulate the answers for ourselves. Do *we* know the answers?

"Where are you?" Adam described what happened step by step. He first heard the sound of God walking toward them. Then he felt afraid for the shame of his nakedness. Finally, he answered the question: "I hid myself." Adam had escaped behind a tree. That's *where* he was.

But the question went much deeper. It wasn't a geographical question, as though the Lord God had lost Adam. It was a relationship question: "Where are you, Adam, in your relationship with Me?"

'Adam missed it. If only he had come out of hiding to answer the question properly: "Lord, I have sinned against You. I have eaten from the tree of disobedience, and I am in sin and separated from You. I don't know what else to do but hide from you. That's where I am." The open confession never happened.

Adam and Eve both stayed in hiding, paralyzed by the fear of glory. This time there were no fig-leaf solutions. They couldn't move—stuck. There was no way to enter back into God's presence.

Only the Lord could provide a way back. Until then, they would remain separated by sin, strangers to His Eden fellowship.

The Fellowship of the Lord Jesus

"I am the way," Jesus taught his disciples, "and the truth, and the life; no one comes to the Father, but through Me" (John 14:6). This is the good news (and it marks the end of all hiding): Jesus Christ came to deal with the separating issue of sin.

It's the great truth of the New Testament: In the Lord Jesus Christ we've been reconciled to complete fellowship with God the Father.

We enter into that fellowship because God, in His grace, has forgiven our sins. He has done this by sending His one and only Son to shed His blood on the Cross of Calvary. Jesus Christ, the Lamb of God, gave proof positive that He has fully dealt with the issue of our sin by His resurrection to eternal life. His triumph over sin and death for all time means that He alone is the way to the Father for all who will receive Him.

Paul said it in other words: "Now all these things are from God, who reconciled us to Himself through Christ" (2 Cor. 5:18). John wrote, "And indeed our fellowship is with the Father, and with His Son Jesus Christ" (1 John 1:3). That is Eden fellowship.

This is the very heart of the Good News: Because of Jesus

Christ and His work on the Cross, our separation from God is over.

The early church came together to celebrate their relationship with the resurrected Christ. They knew the secret of being a *living church*: "For where two or three have gathered together in My name, there I am in their midst" (Matt. 18:20). Church could not be church, the living body of Jesus, without God's fellowship.

Of course, this did not mean Christians were free from acts of sin. But when they gathered together to worship, to hear God's Word and pray, there was opportunity to confess that sin and receive His forgiveness:

> And the blood of Jesus His Son cleanses us from all
> sin ... If we confess our sins, He is faithful and
> righteous to forgive us our sins and to cleanse us
> from all unrighteousness (1 John 1:7, 9).

Embedded in the gospel message is this promise: When we confess our sins, the cleansing blood of Jesus keeps us in constant fellowship with the Lord.

When we don't confess our sin but hold onto it, it is hard to be active in the body of Christ. Although we might be able to play the role of a Christian in front of others, our sin is evident as we gather as the church in the presence of the Lord Jesus Christ. No one else may know what we have done. But in the songs of worship, in the preaching of the Word, and in the corporate prayers of the people, it is impossible to escape the gentle nudging of the Holy Spirit. He is not interested in our playing the Christian role. He convicts us of our sin and calls us to a deep, abiding repentance. In that moment, we face a choice: to either confess the sin or to run away and hide like Adam and Eve.

Christians who opt to stay in sin often wander away. It becomes too difficult to be part of the ongoing church fellowship. Often when individual believers step out on their own, away from the God-community, it's because they want to continue in the unconfessed sin in their lives.

But when groups of Christians wander off, more often than not it is a sign that the serpent deceiver is at work. Like believers bound by sin, those caught in deception also have a hard time staying in the believing community. It's easier for them to meet with others in deception.

And they meet, mostly drawn together by whatever deceptive, look-alike Christian doctrine has captured them. Maybe the group gets bigger. Typically these groups start in the church. But ever so slowly, dialogue breaks down and the group becomes isolated.

Eventually, they break away and start out on their own. A new fellowship is formed, one that looks like the real church! They also meet to worship God, to hear His Word and to pray. But there is one difference. The presence of the Lord Jesus Christ is not there:

> Behold, I stand at the door and knock; if anyone hears
> My voice and opens the door, I will come in to him,
> and will dine with him, and he with Me (Rev. 3:20).

We must not take this verse out of context. The Lord Jesus was not addressing the unchurched. He was speaking to the Christians at Laodicea. So we must ask some unusual questions: Why was Jesus outside His church knocking at the door? Why wasn't He in the gathering of His own followers where He belonged?

Make no mistake: They were meeting without Him. Jesus stood outside the church fellowship, knocking at the door like an uninvited guest. The church meeting went on. The Laodiceans did the right "churchy" things. No doubt they believed Jesus was with them. But they were deceived, out on their own—without Him.

Jesus lifted His voice, but they couldn't hear. Therefore, He called the church lukewarm and demanded repentance. If they refused, He promised, "I will spit you out of My mouth" (Rev. 3:16).

It is God's holy truth: Church cannot be church, the living body of Jesus Christ, without the fellowship of her risen Lord and King.

The deceiver's job is to get believers to do church without the presence of Christ. When it works, the counterfeit appears so real that the deceived truly believe they're in God's fellowship.

In fact, if the deceiver's quite successful, the Laodicean look-alike church will spread and multiply. Over time it will become the authentic church—normal Christianity. And the true church, where the presence of the Lord Jesus is welcomed, will be called fanatical, driven, too zealous, too emotional—abnormal Christianity.

The serpent deceiver loves to create an institutional, godlike religion—one that is a cheap imitation of true faith. Jesus faced that imitation of true faith. He faced that imitation in His own people. And He wept for them:

> O Jerusalem, Jerusalem, who kills the prophets and stones those who are sent to her! How often I wanted to gather your children together, the way a hen gathers her chicks under her wings, and you were unwilling. Behold, your house is being left to you desolate! (Matt. 23:37).

Jerusalem, the headquarters of Israel's living faith in God, had become known as a people "who kills the prophets and stones those who are sent to her!" Their living faith in God had turned sour.

Like Laodicea, Israel had become a worthless religion. They were willing to carry on all the right traditions. But they were unwilling to receive the word of God through His messengers. Nor would they receive His love: "I wanted to gather your children together." Israel had quietly pushed God away. In His name, they performed the religion while the Lord stood outside—uninvited.

This is the deceiver's work—it continues in our generation.

We must never fear engaging in the traditional Christian rituals. It was the regular custom of our Lord to attend the weekly Sabbath liturgy of His time (see Luke 4:16). He Himself instituted the new covenant bread and wine in the middle of the traditional Passover service—which God had put in motion in Exodus 12. Rituals, set in the purposes for which God ordained them, are intended to enrich our worship of the Lord. But when the reason and substance of the traditions is removed, then the danger begins: Rituals are then performed by rote. They no longer become the means to worship the Lord. Instead, they become an end unto themselves, dead and meaningless.

In the midst of our worship and in the practice of upholding the traditional Christian rituals, only one thing is absolutely necessary: The Lord must be with us. We, His people, must come together expecting to stand in the presence of our God and Father, openly participating in His fellowship, just as in Eden!

If we are separated from that fellowship, it means that sin has crept in. And sin always hides from God. Or it means that the deceiver has crept in. It is harder to deal with deception. Those bit by the serpent often devote themselves entirely to their religion. They believe they are part of God's fellowship.

But they are not. Jesus is standing outside the door, knocking.

Abnormal Christianity

I was eating in the cafeteria when I heard a voice from behind me, "Do you know Jesus Christ as your personal Savior?"

I was a freshman in high school. When I turned around, I was amazed to see the senior class president asking me this question. Startled, I fumbled for a minute and then blurted out, "Yes, I am a lifetime Episcopalian." It came out well, and so I smiled.

"Have you ever read your Bible?" he said pounding the issue to death.

"Yes, many times!" I answered, hoping God wasn't listening. Then I did it. Just to get him off my back, I shared my most private secret, something I had known since I was seven but had told no one. "You know," I whispered, "I'm going to be a priest."

Somehow that didn't impress him. "Did you ever do the *Four Spiritual Laws*?" He saw the puzzled look on my face, pulled out a little tract, and taught me how to receive Jesus Christ into my life as my Savior and Lord. We prayed together—then and there.

Some years passed.

I was in college, majoring in religious studies and preparing for seminary. One Sunday afternoon, a friend invited me to go to a "praise service" held off campus. He raved about it.

"Have you ever received the baptism in the Holy Spirit?" he asked cheerfully.

"Oh, Lord," I thought to myself, "there is more?"

When I didn't respond right away, he jumped in, "Then you don't speak in tongues yet?"

What? Tongues? I fumbled for words again.

No one had told me about these things. I had been in church all my life. To me church was a Sunday event, and I knew when to sit, stand, and kneel. It was the building where we went to learn about God. No one talked about accepting Jesus into my life or tongues.

Some years passed.

I was in seminary. I was invited to attend a conference for clergy on spiritual renewal. It was designed to bring pastors into a dynamic relationship with Christ and to empower their ministries in the Holy Spirit. I will never forget that conference, or Fr. Gerald. At the closing service, he gave his testimony.

"My name is Fr. Gerald," he began. He was a stocky older

man with gray-white hair and thick glasses. "I am nearing ... "—his voice cracked and his head dropped—"retirement." He wasn't able to regain his composure. But that didn't seem to matter to him. He went on.

"I have been in the ministry for forty-two years. My every working hour has been devoted to the church. In all those years, no one ever told me I could have a personal relationship with the Lord Jesus Christ. I didn't know the power of the Holy Spirit—until now.

"Oh, I had people come to me over the years. They would ask questions like: 'Fr. Gerald, have you received the Spirit? Are you born again?' And then they'd say, 'We're praying for you.' I would laugh inside. Didn't they know? I'm an Episcopal priest!"

The room fell quiet. "Now I know, Lord Jesus. Now I know." That moment was bittersweet, sweet because now he knew the Lord. Now he was a saved man destined for eternal glory, but he was bitter because forty-two years of ministry passed without knowing Him. All those sermons, all those services, all those years in the church and he never knew the Christ of Christianity.

I never forgot Fr. Gerald's testimony. Oh, how I wept inside that day. The thought of living my life, especially as a priest, and never knowing the fellowship of the Lord Jesus frightened me.

I didn't want to be part of the Laodicean religion that plays church but does not know Jesus as Lord. That's the serpent's religion: the one that hides behind the Eden tree away from the glorious presence of God. Yet, I knew I could have been like Fr. Gerald—a priest somewhere, serving in a church, unaware of the sound of the Savior knocking at the door, waiting to be invited.

127

Thirteen

DIVISION FROM SELF

The Lord: "Who told you that you were naked? Have you eaten from the tree of which I commanded you not to eat?"
The man: "The woman whom Thou gavest to be with me, she gave me from the tree, and I ate (Gen. 3:11-12).

The man finally made his open confession:"I ate." Even then, he would not accept the responsibility for his own actions. It was as if Adam stretched out his hand from behind the tree, his index finger furiously wagging at Eve, saying, "Not me, Lord! There's the real culprit. She's hiding over there!"

Adam lied. It wasn't Eve's fault. He had made the decision to disobey God's Word on his own. But what else could he do? He felt a new, driving self-centered love inside. It demanded he survive.

He quickly professed his innocence: It was the woman. She sinned first. Moreover, "she gave me from the tree." Adam was out to protect Adam, so he savagely blamed Eve.

Then Adam's focus shifted. Suddenly the finger of blame was pointing to its Creator. Adam began treacherously accusing the Lord: Eve is the "woman whom Thou gavest to be with me." He launched his attack toward God, as if to say, "I wouldn't be in this mess if *You* hadn't given *the woman* to me." It was God's fault. It was Eve's fault. It was anyone's fault but his own.

Eve couldn't accept the responsibility either. The Lord God questioned her: "What is this you have done?"

She simply pointed her finger to the empty brush where the beast had slipped away: "The serpent deceived me, and I ate" (Gen. 3:13). Eve had to protect Eve.

Division—again. But this time it wasn't with each other, or God. Sin was working inside, separating Adam from Adam and Eve from Eve. Self divided from self. Sin was rupturing the God-given unity of heart, soul, and mind into shattered bits and pieces.

On one hand Adam loved the Lord. He also loved Eve; she was bone of his bone and flesh of his flesh. But on the other hand, he had turned against both of them, as if they were his deadly enemies.

Confusion raged inside them—like an inner world war.

Their peace of God, which once reigned inside them, was gone. Perfect love had been cast out by fear. Their eternal, God-breathed life had been snuffed out by a new kind of life, an ungodly life, a life with death in it. The image of God in them cracked like a mirror, distorting their image of themselves.

There were no safe trees to hide behind, no fig leaves that would do the trick. They could not run from themselves. Somehow, they would have to develop a place inside—maybe an unconscious world—where they could hide from the internal division of sin.

Self divided from self. It's the way of sin and deception.

Caught in Hypocrisy

"Arise, Peter, kill and eat!" (Acts 10:13). Was it a dream? A vision of some kind? Peter had been staying in Joppa with Simon the tanner. Shortly before lunch, Peter went onto the rooftop, overlooking the Mediterranean Sea, to pray. He felt himself slip quietly into a sleep-like state. That's when he heard the voice.

His eyes opened. There toward the sea, a white sheet like a larger-than-life movie screen descended from heaven. Inside it, a Hollywood movie began to play. The picture? It was filled with animals—animals everywhere! Peter could not believe his eyes.

But the voice told him to arise, to kill and to eat.

Peter was shocked. The creatures in that picture were uneatable. These were the ones ruled unclean by the Law of Moses (see Lev. 11:4). What was the Lord saying? Was God testing him?

"By no means, Lord," he said unabashedly, "for I have never eaten anything unholy and unclean" (Acts 10:14). Peter was confused. Why would God command him to eat contrary to His own Law? As he wrestled with this question, perplexed in heart, the Lord said this: "What God has cleansed, no longer consider unholy" (Acts 10:15).

This vision, from beginning to end, took place three times. After these things, the Holy Spirit spoke to Peter: "Behold, three men are looking for you. But arise, go downstairs, and accompany them without misgivings; for I have sent them Myself " (Acts 10:19-20).

These men had come to take Peter to the house of Cornelius. This man was a God-fearing Gentile who had received a vision from the Lord. In that vision, an angel had told Cornelius to send for Peter and to listen to his message. He sent for him right away.

But there was a problem: Cornelius was a Gentile! To a Jew,

Gentiles were as unclean as the forbidden animals in Peter's visionary movie. Now, suddenly, Peter was being escorted into a Gentile's house to preach the good news of Jesus' resurrection.

The apostle stopped at the threshold of Cornelius's home:

You yourselves know how unlawful it is for a man who is a Jew to associate with a foreigner or to visit him; and yet God has shown me that I should not call any man unholy or unclean (Acts 10:28).

It went against every fiber in his being—but Peter entered the house of a Gentile! He grasped the message of the Spirit in that God-sent movie: "I should not call any man unholy or unclean."

As he began to tell them about Jesus, "The Holy Spirit fell upon all those who were listening to the message" (Acts 10:44). Peter watched in amazement as God confirmed His word: the Gentiles were no longer unclean. The gospel of Jesus Christ was freely open to them.

Now Peter knew. But years later the power of the movie sent from God and the Cornelius experience would slowly fade from his memory.

It happens with the passing of time.

Peter became the chief apostle in Antioch. This church grew in power as Jew and Gentile alike received the Lord Jesus Christ—until, that is, the serpent deceiver came to town—and to Peter.

Religious elders sent from the apostle James arrived with a new doctrine: "Unless you are circumcised according to the custom of Moses, you cannot be saved" (Acts 15:1; see also Gal. 2:11-14). They turned to the Gentile converts in Antioch and demanded they obey the Law of Moses.

Peter was torn inside: These men spoke with authority. They persuasively argued from the Scriptures that the God who gave His only Son also gave Moses the Law, and that Law must be obeyed—even by devout followers of Jesus the Messiah. It sounded right.

Yet, on the other hand, Peter knew what the Holy Spirit had done. He knew the Spirit had fallen freely on the Gentiles—not because they obeyed the Law, but because they believed in Jesus.

Confusion played tug-of-war in his soul. What was he to do? Give in? Let James' men take charge? The moment Peter pulled back and let the new gospel rule in Antioch, division set in. James' men separated Christian Jew from Christian Gentile. Division.

Deception. It took the man Paul to stop the lie in Antioch:

> I opposed him [Peter] to his face, because he stood condemned. For prior to the coming of certain men from James, he used to eat with the Gentiles; but when they came, he began to withdraw and hold himself aloof, fearing the party of the circumcision. And the rest of the Jews joined him in hypocrisy (Gal. 2:11-13).

Paul confronted Peter to his face. Peter knew the truth. He had witnessed the God-movie, the Cornelius story, and countless other testimonies from Gentile converts. God's word was clear.

But the deceiver came. He came dressed with authority from James, the Lord's brother. He came with a reasonable gospel that sounded right and had the power to make Peter believe a lie. And he really believed it. Peter stood condemned. In many ways, the serpent's Eden strategy had worked once again. But this time, the devil in disguise tricked a great apostle into living a lie.

If Peter had any knowledge that his gospel was wrong and still acted on it, then he was not wholly deceived. Deception, in its fullest, does not give its victim the pleasure of knowing that evil is dressed as holy. It is important to see that even if Peter had some inkling that this was wrong, he could not stop it. The new gospel had too much power, it looked too Christian, and Peter fell for it. It took Paul to intervene, save Peter, and strip the holy mask from the devil's unholy face.

The Mask of God

Peter was caught in hypocrisy.

In the Greek world, the word *hypocrite* described an actor, someone acting like someone else. The word was used at social occasions where guests held costume masks over their faces. Their real faces were hidden, like a smiling clown hiding a broken heart.

Satan is the author of hypocrisy. His aim with God's people is to come as deceiver and create religious hypocrisy. He attempts to drive a wedge between what a person believes and how a person behaves—secretly, without them knowing it.

Jesus saw Satan's religious hypocrisy at work: "Woe to you, scribes and Pharisees, hypocrites!" (Matt. 23:23). He knew they were performers: teaching Scripture with their lips but not living the truth with their lives. For this reason, Jesus taught the crowds, "All that they tell you, do and observe, but do not do according to their deeds; for they say things, and do not do them" (Matt. 23:3).

He stripped their hypocritical holy mask away, for they *say* but do not *do*. The serpent deceiver had driven a wedge into the Pharisees, separating their God-talk from their daily God-walk.

That's what happened inside Peter. He believed the Gentiles were free and equal members of the church. But, that's not how he behaved when the deceiver came to town. He put on a religious God-mask. Like an actor, he played the role. A wedge drove deep.

It's the way of sin and deception: self against self.

Peter became lost in confusion. On the one hand, Peter's heart believed God's Word. On the other hand, his mind rationalized the deceiver's logic. It sounded godly. Division was ripping Peter in half. And so he put on the Christian-smiling hypocritical mask.

And like most believers caught in deception, Peter started to live an external Christian life that did not match his inner, real person. He lived in tension, like the war Adam knew inside—blaming God and Eve, yet loving God and Eve. Self was battling self.

This is the great goal of the deceiver—to get Christians to wear the God-mask— outside Christians only. Paul stopped the hypocrisy in Peter. He set the precedent: Oppose the deceptive lie lest we become Christian actors and not real Christian people.

A Leper Without Love

Chris sat in the back—alone.

Everyone seemed happy to see her. Lots of smiles. Some hugs and kisses. There was a wealth of questions: How are you? Is your family well? How's your work going anyway? She didn't have it inside her to smile back or to answer the inane questions. But she did.

It was Sunday morning church.

Model Chris: She had been there five years. It seemed, from the moment she came to this gospel-alive church, she was crowned Miss Perfect Christian. It wasn't hard to do. Chris was a college student then, a stunning woman on fire for the Lord Jesus Christ.

That pizzazz personality! It didn't take the church long to recognize her God-given gifts. Chris was asked to take leadership in the senior high youth group. She stepped in and, in a summer's time, turned those teenagers on for God. Her zeal was contagious.

After graduating from college, Chris joined a New York City advertising firm. In four years, she was made a junior executive. With long ten-hour days, plus the hour-long commute into the city, she still found time and energy to pastor the senior high flock.

She had it all together. Many thought she could do no wrong.

It was our fault. We somehow needed Chris to be that image: Miss Perfection for the younger Christians, and Miss Inspiration of Jesus-fire for the older. We placed that God-mask on her.

I remember Chris came to church one Sunday—a little less bouncy than normal. She was bombarded by people asking, "What's wrong?" Even the pastor called her at home later that evening. In hindsight, I realized it was hard to let Chris have a bad day.

Then it happened. It was really a one-time mistake.

Chris had been dating a well-liked young Christian man for about a year. They were even in the planning stages for marriage. But, one night after a date, their young love went too far. It drove them to see a marriage counselor. They were able to confess their sin, set a marriage date, and vow to cool their passions.

Six weeks later, Chris discovered she was pregnant.

Of course, she turned to her pastor and church in this time of need. She naturally expected to find support and love. But it wasn't there. We were too devastated by the news. We needed Chris (How could she?) to be Perfect Chris. The image was gone forever.

So we put on our Christian mask every time we came in contact with Chris. We smiled and chatted about the weather. We pretended everything was *fine*—as if nothing ever happened. In Christian love, we gave her the cold shoulder. And she knew it.

Yes, of course, we knew the truth. We should have loved and embraced her because God forgives sin in Jesus Christ. But we acted against that belief and behaved arrogantly. We piously judged her a leper, saying, "The Bible says that sex before marriage is sin."

Deceptive religious hypocrisy. Our God-like love mask was a sin. Our prideful self-righteousness was also sin. So was our own selfishness: Our pain in losing the Chris-image was more important than loving the real Chris in her pain. But what could we do?

No one confronted the problem as Paul did with Peter. So we became Christian performers acting out our parts until one day when Chris finally left. And that chapter of our lives closed shut.

Fourteen

REPENTANCE

The Lord said, "For in the day that you eat from it you shall surely die" (Gen. 2:17).

A dam and Eve were dead. God had breathed His life into Adam. When Eve was taken out of Adam, she too had God's life inside her. Together they lived because the original, everlasting life ran through their veins.

Now that breath of God was gone.

In the twinkling of an eye, they were changed. The imperishable put on the perishable, and the immortal put on mortality. Adam and Eve entered a lifeless death kingdom. God said that would happen: "You shall surely die." And they did. They died. They ceased to live in the environment of God's life.

It was a cataclysmic fall. A great and terrible chasm separated creature from Creator—an uncrossable chasm. Only the Lord could rescue them. If He did not intervene, the couple was doomed to live "having no hope and without God in the world" (Eph. 2:12).

But God, being rich in mercy, did intervene.

He began by bringing the serpent deceiver out of the brush: "Cursed are you ... On your belly shall you go, and dust shall you eat all the days of your life" (Gen. 3:14). The Lord cursed Satan, who was hiding inside the serpent. He also cursed the beast Satan used. It would travel on its belly eating dust all its days.

Then the Lord turned to His creation. It was intended to be Adam and Eve's home. From the beginning, God had told them, "Be fruitful and multiply, and fill the earth, and subdue it" (Gen. 1:28).

But now the perfect creation could no longer house the imperfect couple. So the Lord, who spoke creation into being, spoke again: "Cursed is the ground because of you" (Gen. 3:17). An irrevocable curse was place upon the land because of Adam and Eve's disobedience.

From then on the whole of "creation was subjected to futility" (Rom. 8:20). Death reigned everywhere. The physical world no longer ran on the fuel of God's life. It too was part of the death kingdom now, imperfect and marred by the entrance of sin.

Everything changed. The earth produced "thorn and thistle" (Gen. 3:18). The budding flower soon faded, withered, and died; the wolves stopped playing with the lamb and instead killed it for dinner. A fig tree by the Euphrates River stopped bearing fruit.

The new world was a far cry from Eden. Sickness and disease filled the land—war, earthquake, famine, and death itself.

The woman's body was different. She would bring forth children "in pain" (Gen. 3:16). And the offspring were born not in God's image but in the sin-scarred image of fallen man (see Gen. 5:3). We see that distorted image begin with their firstborn son, Cain—the murderer.

The man's body was different. He could no longer garden the perfect earth in the power of the Lord dwelling in him. He was left to till the cursed ground in his own human strength: by the sweat of his face (see Gen. 3:19).

Dust to dust.

But there was hope. God had a plan.

It was a costly plan, designed to bring the creature back to the Lord and His God-breathed life. Adam and Eve would not see the fulfillment of this plan. But they would see its beginning:

And the Lord God made garments of skin for Adam

and his wife, and clothed them (Gen. 3:21).

Somewhere in Paradise an animal died. Its lifeblood spilled onto the ground. The Lord God took the hide from the carcass and "made garments of skin." By His own hand, Adam and Eve were clothed His way—not with man-sewn fig leaves, but with skins from the death and shed blood of an animal. The Lord had begun His saving work.

It was a prophetic statement: God would provide a way back. A day would come when the Lord God would, through the shedding of blood, leap the uncrossable chasm. By His own hand, He would forgive the creatures' sin and clothe them in His paradise garments.

In His saving plan, the door of choice would be open again. In repentance of sin, men and women could opt to live in Eden's God-breathed life or they could choose to remain in their fallen state, dead in their death life—awaiting for the day of judgment and the unquenchable fires.

The God-Breathed Life Restored

It was Sunday evening. The disciples hid in fear of the

Jews. What if someone found them? Would they be crucified too? Condemned for following the Jesus of Nazareth? The doors were shut. Despair filled the room. The women kept insisting He was alive—risen from the dead—but nobody believed them.

No door opened. In an instant He came, stood in their midst, and spoke with that same, familiar voice, "Peace be with you" (John 20:19). The shock! The surprise! The doubt and fear. He was alive—but how was that possible? They had witnessed His death. They had held His body. Could death not hold Him? Then, He lifted His hands. He showed them His side. They kept staring: those pierced hands and feet, His sword scar. That smile. Jesus the Lord was alive. It was Him! It took those few moments but finally, rejoicing filled the room. The disciples burst into the song of Easter—He is risen, hallelujah! Jesus Christ is risen from the dead!

When the songs finished, Jesus huddled His disciples close together. Now it was finally time. The work of the Cross, the very reason He came, was over. The costly plan of redemption was completed. For the first time since Eden, sin and death had been fully paid for by Christ's own blood. The kingdom of God was now open:

> "Peace be with you; as the Father has sent Me, I also
> send you." And when He had said this, He breathed
> on them, and said to them: "Receive the Holy Spirit"
> (John 20:21-22).

Just as God breathed into the Eden couple, so the breath of life was back (see Gen. 2:7). The Holy Spirit had come. The disciples took their first breath in the new kingdom of the beloved Son. In that moment, they were born again. In that place, they became the world's first Christians.

An animal had died. The lifeblood of the "Lamb of God" (John 1:29) had spilled onto the ground. In that one holy act, the Lord Jesus Christ "released us from our sins by His blood" (Rev. 1:5).

The chasm was now crossable. In true repentance, anyone who believed in the Lord Jesus could receive forgiveness of their sins and enter into God's everlasting life. That was His saving plan! But this time He didn't clothe His own in the garments of skin. Instead, the Father now clothed His children in Christ (see Gal. 3:27).

It all made sense Jesus had dealt with sin. Death was conquered. Just as He said, "I am the resurrection and the life; he who believes in Me shall live even if he dies" (John 11:25). Now He could take His followers and, like Adam of old, breathe on them.

The Holy Spirit, God-breathed life of Eden, was back!

He Who Has an Ear—Repent

In Revelation, the apostle John described a vision of seven golden lampstands. In the middle of the lampstands stood the Lord Jesus: "I was dead, and behold, I am alive forevermore" (Rev. 1:18).

Jesus unpacked the mysterious vision: "The seven lampstands are the seven churches" (Rev. 1:20). It was symbolic language. He was standing in the middle of the lampstands— His church! But specifically, He was present to the seven churches in Asia Minor. And He spoke to them with a direct and personal message (Rev. 2–3).

These were His words to each of them: "He who has an ear, let him hear what the Spirit says to the churches" (Rev. 2:7). To be a healthy, alive community in Christ, the Lord Jesus required the seven churches listen daily to the voice of the Holy Spirit.

If they didn't listen, they would allow the deceiver in. And that had already happened.

At Ephesus, the cloaked devil snuffed out the fire of their "first love" (Rev. 2:4). In Smyrna, a group of devout religious believers were nothing more than a "synagogue of Satan" (Rev. 2:9). False teaching has snuck into Pergamum and Thyatira. It was the teaching of "Balaam," the "Nicolaitans," and "Jezebel." Jesus condemned it, for it "leads My bond-servants astray" (Rev. 2:14, 16, 20).

Jesus said the "alive" fellowship at Sardis was "dead" (Rev. 3:1). Although the Philadelphia community had kept the deceiver out, the Laodiceans had kept the Lord Jesus out: "Behold, I stand at the door and knock" (Rev. 3:20). Lukewarm. Bit by the ancient serpent.

His words cut to the quick, like a sharp two-edged sword:
Remember therefore from where you have fallen, and repent ... or else I am coming to you, and will remove your lampstand out of its place—unless you repent (Rev. 2:5).

The Lord Jesus demanded repentance from His people. If a church refused to repent, He promised to remove that church out of its place, just like that.

Why? Because there were no more plans of salvation, no more death and shed blood for sin. The crucified yet risen Savior had fulfilled that plan, once and for all. Now if Christians fall into deception (after being redeemed by the precious blood of the Lamb, Jesus), who will save them? What plan will restore them?

For this reason, the Lord Jesus Christ called the churches to immediate repentance. He did not want Christians, filled with God-breathed life, to have the opportunity to be deceived all over again. By sending the Holy Spirit, Jesus empowered the Christian community to prevent the deceiver from unrelenting havoc. For it is the ministry of the Holy Spirit to guide Christians and the church "into all the truth" (John 16:13).

So the Savior told the secret, "He who has an ear, let him hear what the Spirit says." If the church is listening, the Holy Spirit will enable the elders to spot the serpent of old and stop his work of deception before it's too late, before the serpent bites.

But if the church refuses to listen to the Holy Spirit, the lampstand is extinguished.

The Miracle of Knowing Jesus

I had an appointment at the church at half past two. It was with a young couple in their early thirties, with two children under five. They were new to our church, so I expected this to be a relaxed getting-to-know-each-other time.

We talked small talk: kids, school, jobs. But it fell flat. It was like there was something painful lying just under the surface. But what? I became convinced that Jeff and Debra had come for some other reason.

"We're still confused," Jeff began. "I guess we should start by telling you that Debra's got cancer. It's breast cancer. The doctors believe they have caught it in time. Debra's been through all the tests, and we go in Friday for surgery."

They held their composure like this was old news. There was something else unspoken. I could feel it. As if another bomb with the same destructive power was waiting to fall from his lips.

"We're looking for a new church," Jeff continued.

"Because our church threw us out," Debra said quietly, with a barbed anger.

"What? I don't understand," I responded.

"We were not thrown out—exactly," Jeff interjected. "It's just that we can't stay anymore—as long as she has cancer."

Debra sat straight up in her chair. "Our church believes in the miraculous power of God. I mean, every service is a healing service. And, to be quite honest, sick people just don't fit in."

"Yeah, but we deserved that," Jeff said sharply to his wife. "We did the same thing to people who weren't healed. We made them feel unwanted, like it was their fault for not having faith."

"You're right—that's true." His words disarmed her. "But was it of God?" she asked. "I'd walk out of those services deeply troubled inside, and I would think to myself, 'I'm not coming back here!' But we did, like a magnet drawing us. I don't know why."

"Because we were hooked," Jeff came back. "We wanted to see miracles. I mean—Debra's right. I felt troubled inside too. It bothered me that the pastor never taught the Scripture. He taught only the truths God had shown him about healing through personal experience. The Bible was used only when it proved his point. That should have been a clue to us."

"It was crazy," Debra remembered. "The place was like a zoo. There was never a sense of order. I never felt God's peace. People would go up for prayer and fall to the ground with loud screams of hysterical sobbing or laughter. The pastor would run around with the microphone praying for people. He loved to joke when a miraculous sign happened. He'd say, 'Get 'em, God! Aw'right, Jesus! Do another whopper healing!' It felt almost blasphemous."

"Yeah," Jeff said, "but still, the services were upbeat and full of excitement. They gave us a kind of frenzied high, if you know what I mean. It's like you had to be there."

Hooked. Their voices fell silent as they looked at me. "So they prayed for you and nothing happened?" I inquired.

"That's exactly it," Debra stated. "They told me I needed more faith. Until then, they said, the devil was blocking me from my healing. When they found out I was seeing a doctor and that Jeff and I were talking about surgery, that was it. We were pushed aside." Tears started coming to Debra's eyes. "Now I just don't know what to do. Should I have surgery on Friday or not?"

"Well," I said, the Scriptures say, 'By his wounds you were healed'" (see Isa. 53:5, 1 Pet. 2:24).

"They used that Scripture a lot," Jeff commented.

"And what does it mean? Do you think that always means physical healing? You see, when Isaiah the prophet first spoke those words, he was prophesying about the coming Messiah. His emphasis was that the Messiah Himself would be pierced for our transgressions and crushed for our sins. In the same breath, he said, 'by his wounds you were healed.' In context, the real healing that is promised in Jesus Christ is that He will heal us from the foul, deadly disease of sin. That is what He did on the Cross of Calvary. When we come to faith in Christ, He heals our soul! And, one day when we reach heaven's shore, we will receive a new body where sickness and death will be no more. For now, we have these bodies, but with new, resurrected life in them. We are changed!"

"Now that is healing!" I continued. "The greatest miracle in our lives is to be born again in Christ Jesus our Lord. He breathes His new life, the Holy Spirit, into us, and we enter into the everlasting life of God that never dies."

"Then do you believe God physically heals today?" Debra asked.

"Oh yes, I most certainly do," I answered. "But signs and wonders are meant to direct our whole focus to Jesus Christ alone. Are you aware that Satan also believes in miracles? The Scriptures teach in 2 Thessalonians 2:9 that he even performs miracles, seductive miracles. There is a way to tell when Satan is at work. The signs and wonders become the focus.

"Are you saying there is a counterfeit?" Jeff asked.

"It's true," Debra reasoned, "that everything was focused on miracles. It was always more important than anything else. And because we didn't get our miracle, we didn't fit in anymore. So we fell into a counterfeit, didn't we?"

They sat back in their chairs, and I watched the gentle wind of the Father's peace cover them like a warm blanket covering the sick.

There is a deep pain in the heart when a Christian is rejected by fellow Christians. These two sheep, half-eaten and then spit out, had come to realize the dangers of their experience. It was possible to focus on healing and not the Healer, the miracles and not the God who performs them. They would have stayed at that church had the cancer not come.

In many ways, the cancer opened their eyes to see the ravenous wolf who had distracted them from hearing the true gospel and living for Christ first. The deceiver was trying to steal their hearts away. He was trying to make them feel rejected, faithless, and despairing. No doubt the devil wanted this couple to leave the church and, as Job's wife recommended, curse God and die.

But that didn't happen. Instead, Jeff and Debra recommitted their lives to Jesus Christ, their Healer, that day in my office. Debra went into surgery that Friday. The doctors caught the cancer in time—it was localized. The radiation treatments made the recovery process long. Our church family surrounded them in prayer and in love during those long months.

At last, the serpent liar had fled from their lives.

"Even if I didn't make it," Debra said later, "I knew in my heart that I would have been with Jesus. As they were taking me to surgery, I felt His presence more than I had ever known. And I knew, no matter what, I was going to be all right because He was there with me!"

Jeff and Debra were healed, back into God-breathed, resurrected life in Jesus Christ.

Fifteen

DRIVEN OUT

"So He drove the man out; and at the east of the garden of Eden He stationed the cherubim, and the flaming sword which turned every direction, to guard the way to the Tree of Life" (Gen. 3:24).

It was Christmastide 1974. We were eating lunch on the top floor of Harrods department store in London. A terror-stricken man came screaming into the restaurant. "Oh, God, there's a bomb in here!" Mass hysteria broke out. Thousands of holiday shoppers jammed the stairs and escalators—all of us madly running for our lives.

We were driven out, just like Adam and Eve were driven out of Eden, banished by God's hand. They fled for their lives, for darkness cannot remain in light, and sin cannot stand in God's holy presence and survive.

Before they left, the Lord stationed the cherubim and a flaming sword around the Tree of Life—a cautious, loving act.

For what if Adam and Eve suddenly repented? What if they decided to run to the Tree of Life—and eat—hoping this fruit would forgive their sin and restore them to the everlasting life of God?

Maybe that's what they were thinking.

The result—the grotesque mixture of the forbidden death-fruit and the promised life-fruit—would have condemned them to live *forever* in their sin. For this reason, the Lord stepped in. He blocked the way to the Tree of Life.

Adam and Eve were driven out like common convicted criminals. Exiled from Eden, they came upon a cold, gloryless land.

Did Adam and Eve look back? Did they feel a deep longing to be home again? What went through their minds? They knew they were once creatures of God's paradise who walked daily in His presence, who lived to the praise of His glory, who were appointed to rule over His creation. And what was it like to know it was gone? Gone ...

What would they tell their children? How could they explain Eden-life to a people who never experienced it? Would the children understand? Or would they think that God created the world in sin? Would they blame Him for causing this monstrous life of untold death? And when they grow up, when their young get sick and die in their arms, will they turn against the Lord? Will they say He is unloving? Unfair? Wrong for making a world with immeasurable suffering? Will the children blame the Lord for this fallen world?

The lonely, bitter anguish. What did they say? Did they cry out, "Father, we're sorry. We promise it won't ever happen again. Give us a second chance. Pardon our sin against You."

Adam and Eve knew the justice of God was at work. They were guilty of sin, and God does not wink at sin. If He did, He'd be less than just, less than God. Justice required the penalty due their crime: "The wages of sin is death" (Rom. 6:23). As God said of the knowledge tree, "In the day you eat from it, you shall surely die."

It was a cold, gloryless land.

At some point, the Scriptures do not tell us when or how, Eden disappeared. There is no further mention of the Tree of Life surrounded by cherubim or a flaming sword—no perfect garden of God on planet earth, no Eden where God walks in the cool of the day.

Biblical archaeologists and historians have searched for ancient paradise lost, but no one has found it. It has led some to conclude that the garden of glory was nothing more than myth.

But that's not true. Like Adam and Eve, Paradise too was gone.

Judas

A little boy playing with fire behind Mother's back will be caught eventually. Or worse, he will be burned. Or worse yet, he will start a fire that might endanger the lives of his family and friends. It does not matter how invincible he feels. Little boys who play with fire sooner or later get scorched by fire.

The same is true for a believer who toys with deception. Of course, people don't know when they're being deceived. Eve didn't know. She believed, right up to the moment she ate the forbidden fruit, that the serpent had spoken the truth to her. But when Eve ate, she knew. And it was too late. She had sinned unto death.

So it is for all who are in deception. There is that day, a dreadful and terrible day, when the person being deceived discovers the wicked truth: They have been lied to, tricked, caught in the spider's masterfully spun death-web. And there's no way out.

This is the story of Judas.

It is hard to remember that he was one of the twelve chosen men. Judas lived with Jesus for three-and-a-half years. He watched the miracles, heard all the teachings, and knew what few knew: "Thou art the Christ, the Son of the living God" (Matt. 16:16).

Judas, too, was empowered by the Spirit and sent out to preach the kingdom of heaven, heal the sick, raise the dead, cleanse the lepers, and cast out demons—just like the other eleven disciples.

Make no mistake: Judas was one of them.

We see this clearly at the Last Supper. On the night before His death, Jesus told His followers: "Truly I say to you that one of you will betray Me." The disciples "being deeply grieved" responded by asking, "Surely not I, Lord?" (Matt. 26:21-22). Why didn't they know, or even suspect, that Judas was the betrayer?

And they didn't know. Nor did they have a clue. It was John who wrote, "The disciples began looking at one another, at a loss to know of which one He was speaking" (John 13:22). This Judas was a bona fide disciple, a Jesus-follower, devoted to the end.

Here's the question: Did Judas know he was the betrayer? Or was he, too, at a loss? Did he also ask, "Surely not I, Lord?"

Judas didn't know. Why? Because he was deceived.

The serpent had come to him and whispered a wonderful, godlike plan into his ear. Imagine it: What if Jesus the Messiah was delivered into the hands of the chief priests at the Passover? There was no better time: Jerusalem would be teeming with Jews from all over.

There the Christ would stand for all to see. At that great moment, the Son of God would *have to* prove His Messiahship, bring down the Roman captivity of Israel, step into power, and usher in the kingdom of God, where He would reign forever as King of kings!

This was a glorious plan of God, not a malicious betrayal!

For this reason, when Judas came to Gethsemane with the

Roman officers and chief priests, he kissed Jesus. He still believed his plan was his Father's perfect will. He still loved Jesus even more than ever.

It wasn't until the next morning that Judas learned the raw ugly truth. He had been lied to, caught in the spider's death-web, and deceived by Satan himself. He knew there was no way out:

> Then when Judas ... saw that He [Jesus] had been condemned, he felt remorse and returned the thirty pieces of silver to the chief priests and elders, saying, "I have sinned by betraying innocent blood" ... and he went away and hanged himself (Matt. 27:3-5).

His secret plan from God had failed. The Lord Jesus didn't step into His kingdom. He was sentenced to death, crucified as a common criminal for all to see. Why? What had happened? Judas had listened to the serpent of old. He had come to see himself as part of God's eternal plan to help Jesus step into power. He was driven to be the great mind that would make it all work at the Passover. In the end, Judas may have reasoned, Jesus will thank him for preparing the way of His kingdom.

The plan consumed Judas. He could not see that his heart was altogether contrary to the well-being of Jesus of Nazareth. Nor could he see that he was the betrayer, "the son of perdition," whom the Old Testament had long ago foretold (see John 17:12 and Psalm 41:9). No, he thought he was pleasing God and was one of his favored workers.

Judas was deceived, and he sinned by betraying innocent blood.

It was the day, that dreadful and terrible day when the deceived discover they have been had—tricked into sin, scorched by a death fire. That realization drove Judas to commit suicide. He was driven out—forever.

The Shipwrecked of Faith

151

Alexander was a coppersmith and a prominent Jewish elder in Ephesus. We are introduced to him in Acts 19:33 as a spokesman of the Jewish people, a well-known public figure who tried to bring a chaotic citywide meeting, on the verge of a riot, to order.

We don't know when Alexander came to faith in Jesus. But he did, at least on some level. Nor do we know how long he held onto the faith. But we do know that he announced his conversion to Christ publicly and became Paul's disciple—for a time.

It is thought that Alexander's primary motivation for his new faith was to stay in the public eye, not as a Jewish elder but as a Christian elder. Maybe he even envied the same Spirit-given authority he saw in Paul, full of the lust for power that often opens the door wide for the deceiver (see Acts 8:9-24).

And it did. Alexander got snakebit.

He grabbed onto the latest *new* religious fad-gospel. He became its strongest supporter. He quickly gathered a loyal following, became prominent in the church, and then divided it, upsetting the faith of many—simply by teaching "strange doctrines" (1 Tim. 1:3). He then turned against Paul and vigorously opposed his message. By so doing, he caused Paul "much harm" (2 Tim. 4:14-15). Alexander felt power again.

Paul stepped in. He knew his authority in Christ. These are his words to Timothy, whom he left as chief pastor in Ephesus:

> Fight the good fight, keeping faith and a good conscience, which some have rejected and suffered shipwreck in regard to their faith. Among these are Hymenaeus and Alexander, whom I have delivered over to Satan, so that they may be taught not to blaspheme (1 Tim. 1:18-20).

Alexander's dreadful and terrible day had not yet come. He firmly believed he was a faith-filled Christian who worshiped the true God in Jesus Christ. As one deceived, he was not yet aware that he had rejected faith.

For this reason, Paul drove Alexander out of the kingdom of God, out of Eden, and into Satan's own grasp. He did it out of love—love for the church that was being victimized by Alexander's charisma and false doctrines—and love for Alexander that he might come to Christ rightly and be saved. For this to happen, it was Paul's prayer that pompous Alexander might discover the dark truth: He had been seduced into sin by the serpent, snagged in the spider's web.

Alexander was driven out in the hope that "his spirit may be saved in the day of the Lord Jesus" and that he might humbly repent of his blasphemy before it was too late (1 Cor. 5:5).

The Deceiver and the Making of a God

Erilynne and I called a meeting with Jamie. The Holy Spirit had long gifted her with a healing ministry. She had served three years on our church staff. She was an angelic-looking woman in her mid-forties, kids grown, married to a less-than-enthusiastic Christian man.

"Jamie, we feel it's time for you to take a few months off from ministry," I started. "I say this as your minister, along with the council of elders. We recommend you take some time for yourself, to rest and allow the Lord Jesus to take care of you for a while."

"It's important!" Erilynne said cheerfully. "We burn out so quickly if we don't set aside time for the Lord to minister to us. Everyone who serves the Lord must take that well-deserved rest."

Jamie wasn't prepared for this. It caught her by surprise.

"That's so nice," she said smiling. "I appreciate everyone's concern. Really I do. And you're right. Rest is so important. But quite honestly, I've never felt better. Plus, let me tell you the latest news about my ministry. Last week I was in Cleveland—"

"Jamie," I interrupted, "we want you to clear your calendar immediately. Your peers in ministry all agree on this together."

"I can't. I won't," she said quickly. "I'm ministering with

two bishops on Monday, the third. Then I'm flying to Washington, D.C., for a week-long healing conference. My schedule is booked solid!"

I shook my head. "Jamie, you must listen to us carefully. It's time to rest."

"Oh, come on!" she said in near desperation. "Don't do this. There are so many people out there who need me. I get phone calls every day to go somewhere. I have to turn most of them away. I've really become something special!"

"Jamie, we can't reach you," I said. "And it's not just us. The council of elders, your friends, even your husband are all deeply concerned for you. And we're saying the same thing. You are not listening. Why? I suggest your healing ministry has become more important than anything else in your life. You, your ministry, and where you're going is all you talk about— that plus the great miracles the Holy Spirit has done through you. It's always about *your* ministry."

"Oh, yes it is!" she darted in. "What's more important than serving the Lord Jesus? Really, what else does this life offer?"

"Well," Erilynne said, "I miss you. We used to have a lot of time together. We'd go out to lunch and spend a few hours talking about the Lord, or maybe our kids. We used to be very close friends."

"I know. But I haven't had any time ..." her voice faded.

"It's time to find time," I said, "because there's something greater in life than ministry. It's Jesus Christ Himself and growing in our relationship with Him. It is wanting Him more than what He does through you. Also, by His own command, it's loving His people. It is letting His people care for you too— whether you minister or not."

"I can't believe this," she whispered. "Look, I have got too many speaking engagements right now. I'll pray about it. Maybe in a couple of months—for a few weeks in late summer. How's that?"

"Jamie. It is time to stop," I said quite firmly. "Stop before pride takes root, before you become convinced that you alone know what the Lord wants from you. You must listen to us, to the elders—to your family."

By the time we intervened, it was too late. Her ministry had become her god. We had failed to see the deceiver fast enough. He had come to make her love for ministry replace her love for Jesus Christ. It worked. Jamie was addicted—and she didn't know it.

"I am leaving this church," she announced the next day. "Too many people need my ministry. And I know the Lord has anointed me for a great work. Nothing can stop that, not even those I love."

We were too late. The deceiver had already done his work.

Jamie was out on her own in a cold, gloryless land.

Part IV

THE AWAKENING

Sixteen

PREVENTION AND THE PASTORS

"And now, behold, I know that all of you, among whom I went about preaching the kingdom, will see my face no more" (Acts 20:25).

The elders embraced Paul, kissing him again and again with tears and loud wrenching cries. Oh, the heartbreaking grief of his words. Was it really true? Would they never see his face again?

They held on, not wanting to let him go.

Paul was en route to Jerusalem, where the Holy Spirit had said "bonds and afflictions" (Acts 20:23) awaited him—afflictions that he was sure would lead to his death. Knowing this, the apostle stopped in the port of Miletus, some thirty miles south of Ephesus.

He had to see the Ephesian elders. He had to speak one last word, pastor to pastors, elder to elders, a father's final words to his children. For these were the ones God had given him to disciple in Christ Jesus: a people he had prepared in the Holy Spirit "to shepherd the church of God which He purchased with His own blood" (Acts 20:28). These were the leaders of tomorrow's church.

And what was that final word? What urgent message burned as a night torch in Paul's heart for the next generation of elders?

He had just one thing to say. Paul needed to pass on the secret of being a God-appointed overseer. He knew one of his primary jobs as shepherd was to protect the flock from their archenemy: the wolf-sheep—Satan in disguise, undetectable, dressed as one of us—dressed to kill.

And Paul did his job well. His presence stopped the deceiver. But now Paul's job was over. He knew that after his departure, savage wolf-sheep would storm the church. For this reason, he called the elders together. It was time to teach, time to sound the warning:

> Be on guard for yourselves and for all the flock... I know that after my departure savage wolves will come in among you, not sparing the flock; and from among your own selves men will arise, speaking perverse things, to draw away the disciples after them. Therefore be on the alert" (Acts 20:28-31).

Wolves *will* come in. They will prey on disciples. They will be dressed in costume, arising "from among your own selves." If they're not stopped, the flock won't be spared. For this urgent reason alone, Paul charged the elders to be on guard, to be on the alert.

Paul knew that *preventing deception begins with the pastors.* Wolf-sheep will never invade the body of Christ when the God-tested elders know how Satan the deceiver operates in the church and are continuously on the protective alert.

It was Paul's ministry. Night and day he "did not cease to admonish each one with tears" (Acts 20:31). He testified to the "whole purpose of God" (Acts 20:27) and taught "publicly and from house to house" (Acts 20:20). As he pastored the flock, the apostle kept watch, like a shepherd, ever ready to drive wolf-sheep far, far away.

Now it was the elders' turn.

Paul sailed away having given his final word. As a pastor I am moved by Paul's message. What would have been my last exhortation to the next generation of leaders? Might it have been faithfulness to the Lord, to His Word, to prayer, to the work of evangelism? Would I have encouraged them never to lose heart, to stay the course, to be a model of Christ in their day? For Paul, there were no options.

He was concerned about his flock. He remembered what happened to Eve. He knew the heart and soul of being an apostle of the Lord Jesus Christ meant he must, by definition of that role, issue this one warning. That was Paul's job: to pass on the secret of being an overseer. He had to warn the pastors about the devil in disguise, the wolf in the midst: Be on guard. Be on the alert, for they will come.

Paul's Writing in the New Testament

Paul was father to the newborn churches. "My children," he penned to the Galatians (Gal. 4:19). And to the Corinthians he wrote affectionately, "In Christ Jesus I became your father through the gospel" (1 Cor. 4:15). That father's heart worked hard in the Holy Spirit to "present every man mature in Christ" (Col. 1:28, RSV). He saw beyond evangelism, like a parent sees beyond birth.

Paul's father-mission was for young churches "to grow up in all aspects into Him, who is the head, even Christ" (Eph. 4:15). After all, baby converts must be nurtured into adulthood! If this growth doesn't happen, they will surely be "tossed here and there by waves, and carried about by every wind of doctrine" (Eph. 4:14).

That's why Paul wrote so many letters. It is why he desired

to go back, after founding new churches, and "see how they are" (Acts 15:36). He knew the serpent of old would come, blowing "every wind of doctrine" and upsetting the faith of the young disciples.

Paul was like a father protecting his young. His epistles, nearly all, were written because the deceiver had already done his work. He had come in disguise, made a stand, persuaded the faithful, and wrought sure division in the church.

Paul prayed. He wrote furiously—for them, for us.

He advised the Corinthians: Remember Eve. For Satan appears as "an angel of light." He presents "another Jesus." He baptizes with a "different spirit." But was Paul too late? Had the false apostles succeeded? He feared the worst (see 2 Cor. 11).

In Galatia men had come teaching a "different gospel," convincing Christians to desert Christ (Gal. 1:6). Outraged, Paul called the Galatians "foolish" (Gal. 3:1) and demanded the false preachers be "accursed"—even if they were angels sent from heaven (Gal. 1:8).

Preachers had sprung up in Colossae, men "puffed up without reason" (Col. 2:18, RSV) who had witnessed secret angelic visitations and knew the deep secrets and mysteries of God that no one else knew. They captivated believers with their "self-made religion" (Col. 2:23). So Paul wrote:

> See to it that no one takes you captive through philosophy and empty deception, according to the tradition of men, according to the elementary principles of the world, rather than according to Christ (Col. 2:8).

Paul alerted the Philippians to "beware of the dogs, beware of the evil workers, beware of the false circumcision" (Phil. 3:2). In Romans he urged them to stay away from those who caused "hindrances contrary to the teaching which you learned." They are serpents who "deceive the hearts of the unsuspecting" (Rom. 16:17-18).

In his letters to Timothy, Paul taught the young man how to confront the deceiver, how to correct "with gentleness ... those who are in opposition, if perhaps God may grant them repentance leading to the knowledge of the truth" (2 Tim. 2:25).

This was the man Paul: the father, the God-appointed elder. Whether in person or in letter, his assignment was to protect the flock from the wolf-sheep. For he knew the deceiver and his ways. In every fiber of his soul, he remembered what happened to Eve in the garden of Eden. And he stood watch, lest it happen again.

After his work was completed, the race run, his letters remained. Paul's great apostolic warning was left for elders of all generations to embrace and implement the same work of guarding the church. And then, when their race was over, they could also do as Paul did—pass it on.

The Apostles Peter and Jude

Peter also proclaimed the apostolic mandate: "There will also be false teachers among you, who will secretly introduce destructive heresies" (2 Pet. 2:1). They will "exploit you with false words" and "because of them the way of the truth will be maligned" (2 Pet. 2:2-3).

The second letter of Peter is devoted almost entirely to the warning and prevention of deception. He wrote about the wolf-sheep with urgency because he knew his death was imminent (see 2 Pet. 1:14). This letter was his final word, like Paul's farewell in Miletus. And it was the same exact word, the same warning: Be on your guard.

> You therefore, beloved, knowing this beforehand, be on your guard lest, being carried away by the error of unprincipled men, you fall from your own steadfastness (2 Pet. 3:17).

Peter gave one last warning, for he knew, all too well, about unprincipled men and their power to carry others away with them. He tried to stop the serpent's attack by telling them "beforehand." Peter demonstrates his own apostleship with this warning and his understanding of what it means to be God's overseer.

Jude's letter is the final word of the New Testament before the Revelation. It emphatically repeats the apostolic message. He was driven by the Lord to "contend earnestly for the faith" (Jude 3) for he knew "certain persons" had "crept in unnoticed" (Jude 4).

They were none other than the traditional wolf-sheep, deceivers in the church, who are hidden from view, unnoticed. Jude knew something had to be done. They had to be stopped. His letter rips off their deceptive masks and exposes the infiltrators for what they really are: Satan's messengers.

> These men are those who are hidden reefs in your love feasts when they feast with you without fear, caring for themselves; clouds without water, carried along by winds, autumn trees without fruit, doubly dead, uprooted; wild waves of the sea, casting up their own shame like foam; wandering stars, for whom the black darkness has been reserved forever (Jude 12-13).

What terrifying images: clouds without water, trees doubly dead, wild waves, wandering stars. But there was something even more frightening. These "hidden reefs" were there, at their love feasts!

A ship's captain knows reefs are deadly. It's an underwater ridge of rock or coral that rises near the water's surface. If it is not seen, it can sink the entire ship. And, said Jude, that is what deceivers are: hidden reefs, bent on sinking the church.

Like a ship's captain, Jude kept watch night and day, ready at all times to stop the hidden reefs from capsizing the faithful. That was Jude. That was the New Testament job of God-appointed overseers in the church of the Lord Jesus.

Prevention Begins with the Pastor

It was Sunday morning, November 26, 1989. By half past nine, the high school auditorium in Darien, Connecticut, was nearly half full. By ten o'clock, some twelve hundred people packed the place where St. Paul's Church had met and worshiped the Lord Jesus Christ since the late seventies.

That day was Terry's last day.

For more than seventeen years, the Rev. Dr. Everett "Terry" Fullam was the God-appointed chief elder of St. Paul's. The church flourished under his pastorate. In a mainline denomination, and in an affluent New York City suburb, the Holy Spirit came in miraculous power to renew His church, to save the lost and to glorify Jesus.

Our lives changed forever—and not just ours. Church elders flocked to Darien from all over the world. They wanted the renewing life of the Holy Spirit for themselves and for their congregations—in the hope that their dead churches might come alive.

As Erilynne and I sat in the great auditorium that morning, I wondered to myself, "What would Terry say? What last word would this overseer leave for the congregation and for the elders? What concerns filled his heart? How does a pastor leave those he has loved so dearly?" In the bulletin I saw that the sermon was entitled *Valedictory*—a word meaning "one's closing remarks upon leaving." But what were those final remarks?

We sat on the edge of our seats as Terry remembered all God had done with St. Paul's over those many years. There were so many memories. God the Father had entrusted much to this church. But this sermon was more than a sentimental journey into the past—much more.

Terry had come prepared with a warning. He quoted from Acts 20, when Paul met with the Ephesian elders. Then Terry issued the same warning. He brought the Scriptures alive in our hearing.

A modern-day apostle stood in front of his congregation and said for himself and for the church, "I know that after my departure savage wolves will come in among you, not sparing the flock; and from among your own selves men will arise, speaking perverse things, to draw the disciples away after them." He did not say it might happen. He said it most certainly would happen.

"Therefore, be on the alert." He exhorted the elders to stand united in the Spirit and be on constant guard. For, in Jesus' name, people would rise up the moment he left and try to gain political and spiritual power in the church. They would amass followers, preach false doctrines, and, when strong enough, bring godless division among the faithful. In a short time, the work of God would come crashing down. So with utter seriousness and loving concern, he boldly gave the apostolic charge to the next generation: Be ready. Be on the alert.

The wolf-sheep would most definitely come. We were warned.

The pastor was leaving. His job was over. But that job, the apostolic job of the New Testament overseer, had to continue. And if it did not, look-alike Christian overseers would take charge, deceivers arising from within. And the flock would not be spared.

Terry knew the secret of being a God-appointed overseer. He knew he must warn the pastors, the elders, those raised up by the Holy Spirit and the community to shepherd the church of God that Jesus purchased with His own blood. These must stay on the alert!

Prevention has always begun with the pastor.

If the serpent is going to be stopped, if the savage wolves are going to be arrested, then pastors *must* do their job. According to the New Testament apostles, it is one of their primary jobs.

That apostolic message was Terry's final word. It is always the last word apostles pass on to the next generation of elders.

Seventeen

PREVENTION AND THE COMMUNITY

We have said that preventing deception begins with the pastors. But exactly how do they do that, since wolf-sheep look like real sheep and false prophets sound like God's prophets? What do the elders look for? How does the pastor on the alert do the job? By keeping the church healthy, as a physician keeps a patient healthy.

Just as doctors cannot see the virus invading the patient's body, neither can church leadership see the deceiver virus invading the body of Christ. But doctors know what to do. They watch for symptoms. And when symptoms appear, they fight the sickness head on. In the meantime, their job is to keep the patient healthy and strong.

Pastors must also know what to do. They must watch for the symptoms of deceiver viruses and fight them when they appear. They must know how to drive the deceiver out, and how to keep the body of Christ healthy and strong (as we will see in this chapter). This is God's path to preventing deception.

And it all starts by knowing what we call the "us-language."

That Eden Prayer

Moments before His arrest, the Lord Jesus spoke to His Father. As He prayed for all those who believe, Jesus used a language that hadn't been used since the very beginning of time, words that only someone from Eden would understand.

It is the language of *us*:

> For those also who believe in Me through their word; that they may all be one; even as Thou, Father, art in Me, and I in Thee, that they also may be in Us ... that they may be one, just as We are one; I in them, and Thou in Me, that they may be perfected in unity (John 17:20b-23b).

"We are one," the Son of Man prayed. "Thou, Father, art in Me, and I in Thee." The mystery of the Trinity is great. But the Lord God has always been the *Us* God: perfectly one and, at the same time, perfectly three distinct Persons of Father, Son, and Holy Spirit.

It's the Us-God, after creating the heavens, the earth, and every living creature, that spoke: "Let *Us* make man in *Our* image, according to *Our* likeness" (Gen. 1:26, italics added). And He did. Man was made in the image of God Himself, in the image of *Us*.

But, we might ask, how was he an *us*? That answer is found in the mystery of God's creation of Eve. For when God made the woman, He did not return to the dust of the ground and breathe into a new creature (see Gen. 2:7). Instead, He put the man to sleep—the us-man. From the inside of the us-man, God fashioned the woman (see 1 Cor. 11:8).

166

And the one became two.

Soon after the woman was taken out of the man, God put them together once again through the act of marriage: "For this cause a man shall leave his father and his mother, and shall cleave to his wife; and they shall become one flesh" (Gen. 2:24). Without question, the Us-God had made the us-man like Himself. For the man and woman were two distinct persons but, at the same time, perfectly united as one flesh.

And the two became one.

That was Eden, a place filled with the language of *us*. There was no need to pray that God's people be united. They were "perfected in unity." There was no need to ask that they "be in Us," for the us-man was in the Us-God! They walked as one, knit together in loving fellowship, He in them, they in Him.

But that ended the hour Adam and Eve were driven from Eden. Sin separated them from God. They were no longer in the Us. Sin separated them from each other. They were no longer an us-people. It was gone—the Eden community, the us-image, the us-language—until Jesus prayed the night before His death.

In the Eden prayer, the Savior spoke as one of the Us: "Thou, Father, art in Me, and I in Thee... We are one." Then He prayed that all believers would be an us-people: "That they may all be one ... perfected in unity." Finally, Jesus prayed for the us-people to be in the Us-God: "That they also may be in Us."

In the Garden of Gethsemane, the us-language—the sound that once echoed in the first garden—was back!

The Body of Christ

After hearing Peter's Pentecost sermon the Jews cried out, "What shall we do?" (Acts 2:37). The answer was this: "Repent, and let each of you be baptized in the name of Jesus Christ for the forgiveness of your sins; and you shall receive the gift of the Holy Spirit" (Acts 2:38). Thousands of people came to Christ, received His life-giving Holy Spirit, and were reconciled to the Us-God.

But there was something more. The Spirit of God then placed individual believers into the body of Christ, the church. The result was immediate: "All those who had believed were together, and had all things in common" (Acts 2:44). Christians were together—they were an us-people!

That is always the work of the Holy Spirit. He unites believers to the Us-God. Then He baptizes each and every Christian into the church community (see 1 Cor. 12:13). By His doing, a believer cannot walk alone! To walk with Jesus our risen Savior is to walk with His people. *It cannot be otherwise.*

The New Testament stresses this point. It describes the church as a human body where Jesus Christ is the head. The church is His body, and each individual believer is a body part (see Eph. 1:22). What a perfect illustration of us-relationships!

For a human body to work properly, all body parts must work in consummate harmony. The eye, explained Paul, cannot say to the hand, "I have no need of you" (1 Cor. 12:21). That is absurd! The body must work together with the head. And all body parts "should have the same care for one another" so that "if one member suffers, all the members suffer with it" (1 Cor. 12:25-26). It's how God made the human body work.

And that is how the church in the Holy Spirit works! We are an us-people joined to the Us-God. We are "Christ's body, and individually members of it" (1 Cor. 12:27). We are a people who function together under the lordship of Jesus. Therefore, Paul tells us:

> ... to grow up in every way into Christ, the head. For it is from the head that the whole body, as a harmonious structure knit together by the joints with which it is provided, grows by the proper functioning of individual parts, and so builds itself up in love (Eph. 4:15-16, J.B. Phillips).

This is a healthy church! As we grow up into Christ the Head, we are knit together in that harmonious structure called

His body. By the proper functioning of each body part, the whole body then grows. It grows together, built up in love.

A healthy church is, first and last, a people knit together in Christ's one body, a community of believers in the Holy Spirit who belong to Jesus and to each other. Church is not a building, or a morning service, or an organization. It is a living organism that can only operate "together" under the direction of its Head.

The Church is—and always has been—just like a human body.

Building Up the Body of Christ

The deceiver virus breaks down the body of Christ. It tries to divide the community so that the people of God are not an us-people. It goes after the body parts one by one, rendering them ineffective. It attacks our relationship with Jesus Christ.

But that virus can be stopped.

It is the job of the New Testament elders to keep the church healthy and strong. But what does that mean? It means that their ministry in the Lord is to get each body part working correctly, in agreement with the Head and with the other body parts. Why? So that the body of Christ is working together, built up and ready for service.

The elders are equippers:

> And He [the Lord Jesus] gave some as apostles, and some as prophets, and some as evangelists, and some as pastors and teachers, for the equipping of the saints for the work of service, to the building up of the body of Christ (Eph. 4:11-12).

The Lord Jesus has given elders ("apostles, prophets, evangelists, pastors, teachers") to His church to equip the saints for the work of service. By so doing, the entire community is built up, as Paul said, "to the building up of the body of Christ."

Elders get the body parts working!

It is not that one saint is equipped for service, as if one body part could function alone. How often we see this in our churches! Ministers, and perhaps a few elect lay leaders, frantically try to do all the work of service while the congregation passively watches from the pew. No, God's plan is for every Christian to be equipped. Each person is to be trained to serve in the church community of Jesus Christ as one body. Then they are sent out for the work of ministry—together. The church leadership is given the task of equipping *all* the saints.

This is the Great Commission (see Matt. 28:18-20). The Lord Jesus, before ascending to His Father, gave His disciples the command to "Go therefore and make disciples." Too often this verse is understood only as a mandate to go and evangelize nonbelievers. Without question, Jesus' commission charges us to the great work of evangelism. But it is more; it commands us to make disciples. Biblical discipleship is that great work that takes new believers, raises them, trains them in the ways of the Lord, and equips them by the grace of the Holy Spirit for the work of ministry. The Great Commission emphasizes the work of making disciples.

Paul strove in the power of the Spirit to equip Christians: "And we proclaim Him, admonishing every man and teaching every man with all wisdom, that we may present every man complete in Christ" (Col. 1:28). He got the body parts working.

That is the job of today's elders! By equipping the saints, they build up the body of Christ. Alive—healthy and strong.

Paralyzed

Father Jim stood in the pulpit, cleared his throat, and waited for the congregation to settle in for the Sunday morning sermon.

"As my plane took off for Chicago this past Monday morning," he started, "I felt like a million dollars. I felt special, as if God was smiling down from heaven on me with the thumbs-up sign.

"I felt like a blessed man, like I had finally made it. I'm not yet forty, but I am the rector of a large Episcopal church. I'm a few months away from finishing my doctorate. I know all the right people. I sit on prestigious boards. Older priests turn to me for advice and counsel. My name has been considered for bishop.

"Hey, everybody—I've made it! I am Somebody Special.

"It didn't start out this way. Years ago, when I was called by the Lord Jesus Christ to serve Him with my life, it was enough to pastor a small, country parish. It was an honor to tend His flock. But one day I woke up and I wanted more. I wanted a bigger, better church where I could be a bigger, better priest. I wanted the sweet taste of success.

"And I never stopped—until now. At the conference I went to in Chicago this past week, Jesus Christ confronted me. He used a woman's testimony to get my attention. But this wasn't just *any* woman. She was a quadriplegic, paralyzed from the neck down.

"The woman said to us, 'Look at me! This week we have studied the Scriptures. We have seen the church as the living body of Christ. We have seen how Christians are to function together: as one body under Jesus, our Head. And we have committed ourselves to building up the church and making it alive in the power of the Spirit!'

"'But I want to show you a body that does not work. It is a useless, limp body. It does not know how to take directions from its head. It can't work together. It just lies on a bed, unable to be what it was intended to be. I want you to look at me. Go ahead!'

"'This is *not* what the body of Christ should look like!'

"There was a long pause. She was making us look at her. I could not take my eyes off her corpse-like body. As I looked, I began to weep. I felt my own sin burning in my heart. Why am I driven for success? It was all selfishness and personal ambition. And there, right in front of my eyes, was a living example of the church today. My heart broke, and my little world shook. There, in that moment, the Lord spoke to my heart: 'Which is it, Jim? Have you been called to serve your own ministry—or My church?'

"I said it out loud: 'Your church!' But I knew the question was more demanding than that. He was giving me a choice. I could go on beefing up my own ministry. Or I could repent and turn back to the call He had given me years ago. And I chose, then and there, to repent of my selfish, prideful sin. Oh, I'm ashamed of my sin—ashamed to have made success my god.

"My plane sat on the runway for over an hour last night due to a blinding fog. As I sat on the plane, looking out the window, tears still streaming down my face, I remembered how great I felt last Monday morning. I was Father Somebody Special! But, I will tell you the truth, I was not that same person coming home. I have met Jesus Christ again, and He changed my life—my Lord and my God.

"As I thought about the testimony of the paralyzed woman, I knew His call on my life again, the call to pastor His church, to tend His lambs, to build up His body for the work of service.

"I knew what it meant to be a pastor again."

Eighteen

FOOTPRINTS

There should be no division in the body of Christ. The Holy Spirit's ministry is to unite believers. He brings us together with "one mind" (Acts 2:46), with "one heart and soul" (Acts 4:32) so that with "one accord" we might "with one voice glorify the God and Father of our Lord Jesus Christ" (Rom. 15:6).

He fuses us into a bonded fellowship—and makes us one.

At all times, the apostle Paul encouraged young churches to stand "firm in one spirit, with one mind, striving together for the faith of the gospel" (Phil. 1:27). He insisted they preserve "the unity of the Spirit in the bond of peace" (Eph. 4:3). For he knew that when the unity of the Holy Spirit is not maintained, division spreads like gangrene. It scatters the one people into separate camps. It breaks down the body of Christ like a deadly disease.

Division: It is the footprint of the invisible deceiver. It is the one key symptom that announces the deceiver virus has entered the body of Christ. Therefore we can state this as an overriding principle: To see division in the church is to see the deceiver at work. Knowing this biblical truth, Paul acted the moment he knew division was in the air:

> I appeal to you, brothers, in the name of our Lord Jesus Christ, that all of you agree with one another so that there may be no divisions among you and that you may be perfectly united in mind and thought. My brothers, some from Chloe's household have informed me that there are quarrels among you. What I mean is this: One of you says, "I follow Paul"; another, "I follow Apollos"; another, "I follow Cephas"; still another, "I follow Christ." Is Christ divided? (1 Cor. 1:10-13, NIV).

There was division in Corinth. The church was being ripped into pieces by "jealousy and strife" (1 Cor. 3:3). Quarrels had split the church in Corinth into four opposing camps. Christians had turned against each other in the name of Paul, Apollos, Cephas, and Christ.

Paul issued his appeal. He wrote in the name of our Lord Jesus Christ that the faithful preserve the unity of the Spirit. They were to agree with one another and be perfectly united in mind and thought. There should be no division among them.

But there was division. So Paul asked, "Is Christ divided?"

It is a logical question. If my body was sick, people would say, "Thaddeus is sick," for they know that my body and I are one. That's Paul's point. Jesus and His body, the church, are one. So, he asked, if the church is sick, does that mean Christ is divided?

"No!" we might respond, "Jesus cannot be divided!"

But the questions remains: If the Lord Jesus and His church are united together in the Spirit, how can there be division?

The Scriptures teach us that there should be no division. For this reason, the elders are to preserve the unity in the body of Christ. They are to "watch out for those who cause divisions" and keep away from them (Rom. 16:17, NIV). For nothing should be allowed to drive the Spirit's unity from the church—nothing!

Division: It marks the deceiver's presence.

The Council at Jerusalem

The letter began this way:

> The apostles and the brethren who are elders, to the brethren in Antioch and Syria and Cilicia who are from the Gentiles, greetings. Since we have heard that some of our number to whom we gave no instruction have disturbed you with their words, unsettling your souls" (Acts 15:23-24).

The apostles and elders had gathered in Jerusalem. Severe trouble had erupted throughout the Gentile churches in Asia Minor. A confusing new gospel was being taught, disturbing the brethren and unsettling their souls.

These preachers were believers in Jesus. But they were also former Pharisees. Their teaching was an odd combination of gospel faith with the Law of Moses. The power of their words struck the non-Jewish community the hardest since they required that all male Gentile converts become circumcised: "Unless you are circumcised according to the custom of Moses, you cannot be saved" (see Acts 15:1). The result was divisive, separating Gentile from Jew in the church.

Paul and Barnabas vehemently opposed this new teaching on circumcision (Acts 15:2). "There is neither Jew nor Greek, there is neither slave nor free man, there is neither male nor female; for you are all one in Christ Jesus" (Gal. 3:28). But their words on being "one in Christ" didn't stop these preachers.

Division mounted quickly.

Something had to be done. It was time for the elders to recognize that this new gospel was effectively dividing the church. It was time they come together to "look into this matter" and seek the mind of God, so that the division might end (Acts 15:6).

They met in Jerusalem. There was "much debate" (Acts 15:7). James, the Lord's brother, had been associated with the circumcision party. But he listened intently as Peter gave his testimony of all the Lord had done in bringing the Gentiles to complete faith in Jesus Christ. Peter boldly took his stand: "He [God] made no distinction between us and them, cleansing their hearts by faith" (Acts 15:9). Again he testified, "But we believe that we are saved through the grace of the Lord Jesus, in the same way as they also are" (Acts 15:11). Circumcision was no longer required.

Paul and Barnabas also told the gathered assembly all the signs and wonders God had done in the Gentile churches. When they finished, the reputable James stood up with the Scriptures in his hand. The prophet Amos had given witness of the same truth. James' ears were open to the working of the Holy Spirit. Through the testimonies of God's mighty work with the Gentiles and the confirmation of His own holy Word, James' own heart and mind were changed. He realized the truth the Lord was presenting to the church. He knew the division had to stop.

"Therefore," the Lord's brother began, "it is my judgment that we do not trouble those who are turning to God from among the Gentiles" (Acts 15:19). What a statement for James to make! The Holy Spirit had clearly spoken to the assembly. He brought the "apostles and elders, with the whole church" (Acts 15:22) to one mind: Jew and Gentile are one in Christ!

The decision had been made. The elders sent a letter to the Gentile churches in Asia Minor by the hands of select men:

Since we have heard that some of our number to

whom we gave no instruction have disturbed you with their words, unsettling your souls, it seemed good to us, having become of one mind, to select men to send to you... For it seemed good to the Holy Spirit and to us to lay upon you no greater burden (Acts 15:24-25, 28).

When this letter was read to the Gentiles, "they rejoiced because of its encouragement" (Acts 15:31). The day of division was over.

The apostles and brethren had withheld their blessing from the preachers of this new gospel. The elders also rejected their teaching by laying on the Gentiles "no greater burden," not circumcision, and not the Law of Moses.

At the council in Jerusalem, they had become of one mind. Their decision (it seemed good to the Holy Spirit and to us) preserved "the unity of the Spirit in the bond of peace" (Eph. 4:3). Now the Gentile churches could act on that decision: first, by dismissing the division makers and second, by regaining the Spirit's unity.

The division was over. The church of the Lord Jesus was one again.

A Commitment to Unity

The New Testament apostles understood this truth: to see division in the church is to see the deceiver at work. "These are the men," Jude wrote of the wicked deceivers who had snuck quietly into the church "unnoticed" (Jude 4), "who divide you, who follow mere natural instincts and do not have the Spirit" (Jude 19, NIV).

The deceiver is always the divider.

It has been that way since the beginning. The Satan serpent came to Eve when she was alone. He sang his godlike song and led her to the tree of disobedience while the man was out tending the garden. By the time Adam came back, it was too late. The deceiver had done his work. Eve was divided from God and from her husband.

He's the division maker. He comes to the church community to snatch Christians away one by one. If no one notices his work, he causes a divisive faction in the church, one that appears godly, rests on Scripture, and takes the unity of the Spirit away. Sometimes these factions develop as a result of petty, insignificant issues. But the result is the same—division.

For this reason, the council of Jerusalem met! The scent of serpent-like division was in the air. The elders came together to seek the mind of God. Once the Spirit brought them to one mind, they knew they had spotted the garden serpent of old. They intervened quickly, stopping the division and therefore the deceiver.

They were committed to unity.

In the early church, unity was a way of life. Believers met together "day by day" with "one mind" (Acts 2:46). They constantly devoted themselves to "the apostles' teaching and to fellowship, to the breaking of bread and to prayer" (Acts 2:42). They were God's community, baptized in the Holy Spirit's Pentecost power and life.

The Spirit of God makes all the difference! He's the unity-giver. He's the One who brings the faith community into "the same mind, maintaining the same love, united in spirit, intent on one purpose" (Phil. 2:2). His person and presence is the bond that makes us one.

When the elders are committed to that unity, then they will know when division begins to spread through the church. They will know when one sheep among the ninety-nine (see Luke 15:4) wanders away from the flock—off by itself, alone and unprotected.

They will know! For the unity of the Spirit will be gone.

At the scent of division, the elders must come together and seek the mind of God. In that process, the church leaders might discern the division is not the deceiver at all. Problems arise in the life of a church all the time. It may well be the result of miscommunication, a word misspoken or heard wrongly. It might be someone vigorously putting forth their own agenda, completely unaware that they are hurting others. These are only the daily trials of being together as a church family and are not the work of the serpent of old.

But it might be the serpent. So the elders gather together, pray, reason, and discern together. It must be the trust of the gathered leadership that the Holy Spirit will meet with them and draw them together in His unity. And if they discern that it is the serpent of old, it's the elders' duty to intervene and confront the division, and the deceiver, head-on.

There have been times that we have witnessed elders come to a unanimous position—and the division remains. It is possible for a group of Christians who love each other in Christ to come to the same opinion. This is not the same as the Holy Spirit bringing a people into His will and plan. This can be tested by asking, Did our decision arrest the division in the church? Does our decision move contrary to the Scriptures? Did some of the elders feel they were urged to agree rather than express concern and doubt? In such circumstances, the elders must recommit to a time of prayer and fasting, urgently seeking together the will of the Lord for their church.

Division: It marks the deceiver's presence. Unity: It marks the Spirit's presence and is the sure path to preventing deception.

Spot and Stop

The vestry (our board of elders) at Prince of Peace Church decided to attend a healing conference in October 1989. We needed time to be together, and this seemed like the perfect opportunity.

John and Harriet Rucyahana joined us. John is a priest and

an evangelist in the Anglican Church of Uganda in East Africa. He was on a two-year sabbatical leave to study at an Episcopal seminary in Ambridge, Pennsylvania. The Holy Spirit had bonded this couple to our parish—and our hearts.

I remember that first night. We heard the main speaker give a rousing message on the power of the Lord in healing. At the end of his talk, he invited the sick to come forward for prayer. Near the end of the service, I noticed about half of our vestry seemed moved by the Spirit—but half were not. On the drive home, Erilynne and I had the same personal reaction. The night was a mixture of blessing and confusion. It was the first time I had seen such a mixed reaction in our leadership. But I remained confident that God would continue to work the next day—that dreadful next day.

About halfway through the morning session, I looked over at the members of our vestry and I knew something was wrong. Some were lost in prayer while others were looking at their watches and fidgeting in their chairs.

A young man had his hands raised in worship while the older man next to him sat stone-faced, his eyes bulging red with anger. Two women were weeping in each other's arms. I could hear a couple bickering back and forth in loud whispers. Harriet Rucyahana had fallen to her knees. She sensed a great confusion in the church and was fervently petitioning the Lord Jesus Christ to remove the tension.

Something was surely wrong. I stood up and motioned for the group to follow me. We left the meeting and found a quiet room.

"What's going on?" I asked. In a matter of seconds, we were in a heated debate. After ten minutes, two groups had formed: one upset that we had left, the other refusing to go back. One felt they were being blessed by the healing ministry. But the other felt there was a lack of order and a reigning sense of confusion. Both groups were upset with each other. They both justified their positions by referring to Scripture to prove their point.

A heavy cloud sat over us. We were a divided people.

"May I say something?" Fr. John asked holding his hand high in the air. "My brothers and sisters," he began, "it's good for us to hold different views. Our Father has not made us as robots. We are meant to think, to speak our own opinions, and to reason with creativity and variety. But we must be careful! Our opinions must never be more important than our fellowship together in Christ."

"Look here!" the African continued, "Any time confusion steals the peace of God away, we must stop and seek His peace. Any time our own 'right' position is more important than the love of God, we must stop and seek His love. Anytime division separates us from the unity of the Spirit, we must stop and pray for the Spirit of God to drive the division away and restore our hearts into the unity only He can give. Do you think we can do that right now?" he asked calmly.

His words dripped like a healing balm over each one of us.

We sat quietly those next few minutes. Just then, our opinions of the conference didn't matter. Our relationships mattered. We spent the next few hours together, talking, praying, and seeking the Lord with open hearts.

During that time, we came to understand when the division began, and why. We discerned together where the deceiver had snuck into the services and caused a confusion that could be felt by some and not by others. As a result, we as a people became divided. We realized then and there that we had spotted the deceiver. He alone is the author of such confusion and division.

From that moment on, we were able to enter into prayer for the leadership of the conference and for those attending. We returned as intercessors, knowing how to pray and how to stay alert for the marks of the devil in disguise. Together, we saw our divisions cease and the Holy Spirit remove the dark, heavy cloud from our vestry.

We were one again in the Lord Jesus.

REMEMBER EVE

I saw the deceiver's footprints that weekend, splitting and dividing the faithful into separate camps. It has been his work since Eden. His footprints have never changed—never. And once again, I knew the truth of Scripture alive in our day: Spot the division—stop the deceiver.

Nineteen

INTERVENTION

"He who is a hireling, and not a shepherd, who is not the owner of the sheep, beholds the wolf coming, and leaves the sheep and flees, and the wolf snatches them, and scatters them" (John 10:12).

It's a choice. The sheep-watcher "beholds the wolf coming." He knows the wolf snatches and scatters sheep. So what will he do? Will he protect and save the flock by confronting the sheep's killer face-to-face? Or will he avoid the conflict by fleeing?

The hireling, Jesus taught, flees. He's not a shepherd. He runs off because he's "not concerned about the sheep" (John 10:13). He would rather save himself than risk his own life. But the shepherd never flees. He lays down his life for the sheep (see John 10:11).

Should we allow the wolf to snatch and scatter? It's a choice sheep-watchers face today in the church.

Warn with Love

Parents must have a strategy for raising their children in days like these. If they do not, the teenage years will come, and they will not be prepared for the peer pressures, the temptations to explore what must never be explored, and the rebellious independence that separates parents from their young.

I spoke in front of four hundred juniors and seniors at a local high school. It was their kickoff campaign for "No Drinking—No Drugs" at the May prom. I asked them two questions: "Is it wrong to break the law?" I got very little response. "Or is it wrong to get caught?" The auditorium burst into applause, some stood and cheered. That was the game: Do whatever you want to do—just don't get caught.

This attitude, prevalent in all spheres of our society, is what young parents fear the most. As the teenage years approach, theirs must be an intentional strategy to protect the young, or they will lose them. One day, the child will come home from school, eyes blank, hard-hearted, and distant and cold in manner. The parents will reach out to intervene, but it will be too late.

The rebellion has begun. The parental authority has no more weight. A mother's heart, a father's compassion, cannot stop the drugs, the sex, the cursing, the wild life.

Parents must have a strategy. From the early days, unbreakable bonds of trust must be carefully woven into the relationship. And there must be warning—before it happens. The parents of today must slowly, methodically love their children into seeing the dangers ahead of them. The arms of protection must embrace the child before the storm hits. The child must be ready, prepared.

It's hard to do. We want to keep the children forever children. Why break their innocence? Why not let them run and play, free and happy, while they still can? Later we will tell them of the evils they must face in the world. That's how we think. We put off till later what must be done today. Love warns beforehand, before it's too late.

Beware of the false prophets, who come to you in sheep's clothing, but inwardly are ravenous wolves... For false Christs and false prophets will arise and will show great signs and wonders, so as to mislead, if possible, even the elect. Behold, I have told you in advance (Matt. 7:15; 24:24-25).

Jesus warned His disciples in advance. Before the serpent emerged from the brush. Before the false angel of light appeared in a heavenly vision. Before the wolf-sheep entered the community of the shepherd.

He said, "Beware." He told them how deceivers work, what to look for, and why. Without doubt, wolves will come to you. They will arise dressed in disguise, in sheep's clothing: prophets of God; miracle workers. But they will be false. They'll try to mislead the elect. The disciples had to know, fear, and watch.

Love warns beforehand.

It is as if the shepherd took His sheep aside and said: "Stay together and don't wander off alone. Don't form divisive groups. Remember the story of Eve. The wolf will dress like one of you. But here's how you'll know..."

God's chosen elders must have that kind of shepherd love. If they do, they will warn their flock in advance. They'll set the Christians' hearts aflame with the fear of the Lord—that right kind of fear that makes us stay alert, watchful, and safe from ravenous wolf-sheep.

A love-warning. It belongs in the pulpit, before he comes.

What to Do When the Wolf-Sheep Comes

When the deceiver is spotted in the church, the elders have a three-fold mission: 1) to confront the wolf-sheep, 2) to alert the flock by spotting the wolf-sheep for them, and 3) to care for those already caught in the deceiver's grasp. Let's look at it in specific detail.

Confronting the Wolf-Sheep: Action is the first step. The

elders must go eyeball-to-eyeball with the deceivers. It is their job to yank off the religious sheep-costume, to expose and oppose the lie, and to call the persons involved to repentance in Jesus' name.

Many people avoid confrontation at all cost. It is hard to deal with a difficult matter straight on. There is always the dreadful risk of getting hurt, being rejected, or facing an uncontrollable emotional outburst. So we avoid the encounter hoping the problem will take care of itself. This was the sin at the Thyatira church:

> But I [Jesus] have this against you, that you tolerate
> the woman Jezebel, who calls herself a prophetess,
> and she teaches and leads My bond-servants astray.
> ... And I gave her time to repent (Rev. 2:20-21).

Jezebel was a wolf-sheep—a false prophetess and a false teacher. She was *in* the church, teaching and leading Christians astray.

The Lord Jesus held the church at Thyatira accountable. Instead of confronting the deceptive lie, they allowed her ministry to continue: "You tolerate the woman Jezebel." Jesus Himself stripped off her religious mask, exposing her as a false prophet, and called her to repentance. He confronted the wolf-sheep!

Paul exhorted young Timothy to do the same thing. It is the job of the "Lord's bond-servant" to correct "those who are in opposition, if perhaps God may grant them repentance leading to the knowledge of the truth, and they may come to their senses and escape from the snare of the devil, having been held captive by him to do his will" (2 Tim. 2:25-26). Action. It's the first step.

The shepherds must confront, face-to-face.

Alerting the Flock of Wolf-Sheep: Instruction is the second step. The elders must go eyeball-to-eyeball with the church. It's their job to help believers see the deceiver's mask: "Look here," they might instruct, "this isn't a sheep. This is a wolf. Stay away!"

Most New Testament epistles were written for this very

purpose. Wolf-sheep had come into the churches. "These things I have written to you," John emphasized, "concerning those who are trying to deceive you" (1 John 2:26). To the Thessalonians, Paul penned: "Let no one in any way deceive you" (2 Thess. 2:3). To the Galatians: "You foolish Galatians! Who has bewitched you?" (Gal. 3:1, NIV). To the Colossians, "See to it that no one takes you captive through philosophy and empty deception" (Col. 2:8). The list goes on.

The point is made: Shepherds always alert the flock.

The apostles proclaimed a twofold message to the churches: Unmask the deceiver and strengthen the believer. Jude's letter is one example among many. He first exposed the masked enemy: "These are the ones who cause divisions, worldly-minded, devoid of the Spirit." Second, he encouraged the faith community: "But you, beloved, building yourselves up on your most holy faith; praying in the Holy Spirit; keep yourselves in the love of God" (Jude 19-21).

Unmask and strengthen, lest the wolf snatch and scatter.

Deception is built on disguises. But if the mask fails, deception fails and the deceiver loses his power. Surely when Satan "disguises himself as an angel of light", he wields power in the church (2 Cor. 11:14). But the moment he's exposed and angel light turns to angel dark, the deception is over. The faithful see him as he really is, and they turn away. His power quickly disappears.

It is the work of a shepherd to strip away the sheep-mask, to alert the flock, and to build up the church of Jesus Christ.

Caring for Those Caught in the Deceiver's Grasp: Compassion is the third step. The elders must go eyeball-to-eyeball with the deceived, those victimized by the deception. It's their job (with the church) to love them back to health in the Lord Jesus.

This requires the heart of a shepherd. It demands the sickly be strengthened, the diseased healed, the broken bound up, the scattered brought back, and the lost found (see Ezek. 34:4). It's the compassion our chief shepherd, Jesus, felt when He saw the multitudes "distressed and downcast like sheep without a shepherd" (Matt. 9:36).

It is how Paul felt when he spoke "the truth in love" to Peter (Eph. 4:15). He "opposed him to his face," for Peter had been caught in deception (Gal. 2:11). But Paul went to him and brought back the lost. "Above all," Peter would later write from his experience, "keep fervent in your love for one another, because love covers a multitude of sins" (1 Pet. 4:8). He knew this firsthand.

The shepherd and the community stand alongside those caught in the look-alike truth and love them to health. It is more than correcting doctrine. *It's abounding love!* For deception blinds. And that blindness is not always healed right away. Even when the wolf-sheep is exposed, those who have fallen victim to the power of deception may not understand yet.

Yes, they must be loved back into the truth and mercy of our Savior.

But some will not respond to that love. They will remain in the deception, unable to hear God's Word, unable to see even when Satan is unmasked. Some remain caught. It doesn't matter how hard the faithful love; at some point, those blinded by the deceiver will leave the church. (We'll discuss this in the next chapter.)

It is painful to watch people leave, knowing they remain tricked by false teaching. But we as Christians, no matter what, must be faithful to this truth: Compassion cares for the caught.

Remember the example set by our Lord Jesus Christ: Love warns beforehand. It is action that confronts the deceiver. It is instruction that alerts the flock. It is compassion that cares for those blinded by the white lie. This is the shepherd's heart, not the hireling, that loves the sheep with the love of the Lord.

Peter upheld these truths in his last recorded words. They capture the impassioned love-cry of a shepherd for his flock.

You therefore, beloved, knowing this beforehand, be
on your guard lest, being carried away by the error of

unprincipled men, you fall from your own steadfastness, but grow in the grace and knowledge of our Lord and Savior Jesus Christ. To Him be the glory, both now and to the day of eternity. Amen (2 Pet. 3:17-18).

The Choice to Love

"Let there be no division among you!" These were my closing words as a guest preacher in a large Virginia church. Afterwards, Erilynne and I were asked to pray for those in need. Music filled the church. Motion circled around us as people came forward for communion. At some point, a handsome couple stood in front of us.

"I'm Charlie Thatch. This is my wife, Liz," the man said in a low, dignified voice. The couple looked to be in their late fifties. "About ten months ago, we were asked to meet with the board of elders. We've both sat on that board a number of times before."

"We love Jesus," Liz began, her eyes wide open and brimming with tears, "and we love this church. It's been our home for over seventeen years. But right now, we just don't know where to turn.

"It's my fault," she continued. "Two years ago I heard about this prayer ministry out of Texas. I got their books and tapes. Charlie and I were really excited about it. We flew off to one of their seminars where they trained us to lead prayer ministry in our own churches. So, we started to practice that ministry here."

"In hindsight," Charlie came in, "we should have gone to the board of elders and presented it to them. But we didn't. Instead, they called us in. First, they told us our new ministry was causing disruption in the church. And second, they had researched the Texas outfit. Their findings were shocking! From the Scriptures, the pastor gently showed us the deceptive scam of this ministry. We listened and prayed about it. At their next meeting, we formally renounced this ministry and asked their forgiveness."

"But that was it!" Liz said sharply.

Charlie dropped his head. "It's like they decided to cut us off," he said. "Yes, we made a mistake. But not to receive us back? To turn away from us? Not to speak to us? When we understood what was going on, we went directly to the minister and to each member of the board. Nothing. They smiled us away, as if we were making it up. Do you see? It's been such a difficult time. We feel as if we've been rejected by our family in Christ."

"I thought it was all in our head," Liz went on, "like we had a complex or something. But no, it was not. Three months ago my mom died. It was a sudden death and a deeply painful loss for me. Naturally, I called on our minister and asked this community of believers to hold us up in prayer."

"We never received a phone call," Charlie said. "No one from the church came to the house or the funeral. Nobody sent flowers or cards. Their silence said more than we ever thought possible.

"I don't know why we keep coming back," he said ruefully. "I guess we hope it will be over soon. I feel like saying, 'Okay! We're sorry! We sinned. We were wrong. But is that any reason to abandon us? Does God give you the right not to love us? Does He?'"

What torment they felt—abandoned, removed from the love of God's community.

It was not enough. Yes, the elders spotted the disruption in the church, and they stopped it. They found the new doctrine on prayer to be false and they confronted Charlie and Liz about it.

But that wasn't enough. It is never enough.

Without love, the words of warning and correction are heard as unrelenting judgment: *"You are wrong!"* Wrong with no chance to be forgiven—wrong, and only loved when right.

When it comes to stopping deception, *love must abound!*

Twenty

THE CLOSED EAR

"As He [Jesus] said these things, He would call out,
'He who has ears to hear, let him hear'" (Luke 8:8).

To hear—but not to hear. Sometimes stopping deception doesn't work even when all the right steps are taken. There are some who remain deceived. Though the sheep-mask has come off the wolf, they cannot see. Though the elders have cried out the warning, they cannot understand. Though the community of faith has come alongside and tried to love them in their time of deafening deception, they cannot hear.

Helplessly, the church stands by.

Hearing, but not hearing, is a common phenomenon. A husband and wife sit in the pastor's office with years of unresolved hurt between them, never discussed.

"He doesn't listen to me. He doesn't care," she cries aloud as he blankly stares out the window.

"That is mutual," he responds in a monotone laced with anger. "You don't know me at all. You talk to me in that patronizing voice as if I were ten. Maybe I've got needs too! It's not just me. You don't listen."

To hear—but not hear.

Teenagers often tune out their parents. Alcoholics rarely hear anyone who says, "You've got a problem." The absolutely right arrogantly dismiss anyone else's point of view. It is a learned art: We hear what we want to hear. We tune out the rest.

Sin by definition always deafens the ears. Christians will experience the pangs of guilt after committing an act of sin. But what should we say about the second, third, or fourth time? The guilt lessens in strength. The constant practice of sin makes sin easier—maybe eventually "right."

The ears become dull (see Heb. 5:11). Candidly, Jesus addressed the question, "What happens if a believer is caught in an act of sin?" His primary concern: Can they still hear or not?

> And if your brother sins, go and reprove him in private; if he *listens* to you, you have won your brother. But if he does not *listen* to you, take one or two more with you, so that by the mouth of two or three witnesses every fact may be confirmed. And if he refuses to *listen* to them, tell it to the church; and if he refuses to *listen* even to the church, let him be to you as a Gentile and a tax-gatherer (Matt. 18:15-17, italics added).

Ear testing begins in private, then to two or three witnesses, and lastly to the church itself. Each step is an effort to help the brother listen. Why? The objective is clear: to help him hear so that in hearing he might be won. Only those who are truly deaf ("If he refuses ...") fail the test.

Our Savior's words sound cold, dramatic: "Let him be to

you as a Gentile and a tax-gatherer." Does this mean we throw them out of the church? Treat them with scorn? Not speak to them? Yet, how did the Lord Jesus Christ handle Gentiles and tax-gatherers? Didn't He direct His entire ministry to such people, the lost, the sinners? And didn't He charge His church to carry on that same work—to reach those who cannot hear the gospel message?

So our Savior's words are not cold. They are filled with passionate longing for the brother who cannot listen: Treat that person with the kind of love with which you treat a nonbeliever. And let your words and your conduct radiate the love of Jesus Christ that, in the end, they might be won.

This process of helping fellow Christians to hear is more difficult when it comes to deception. Even though sin appears in a godlike disguise, the ears become just as dull. But here is the shocker! The deceived do not know they are in sin or feel its guilt. Instead, they feel right before God, maybe even confident.

The ear-testing process begins. The mask comes off the serpent of old. The elders alert the faithful. If some cannot listen, then the church covers them in prayerful love, with the hope that the non-hearing will soon hear—and be won in Jesus' name.

At some point, those who can't hear will make a decision to follow the deception and therefore leave the church. No amount of love or persuasive argument or prayerful intervention will suffice. The church must let them go. The door will be opened by their own initiative, and the deceived will be gone. Just like that.

It's all in the ears.

When the Church Can't Hear

There are times when it all turns upside down.

Martin Luther stood up in his generation, one voice against the whole of the church. Is it possible that one man is right and the whole church is deceived? Could the church lose its hearing? Is it possible that the church might be unified in being and purpose, upholding mutual love, directed in mission to the poor and suffering—and be wrong?

Tim and Sandy Zimmerman found out it was possible. We met them at a conference just outside Chicago. For eleven years, they attended St. Jude's, a church with two hundred families, a vibrant preacher, and a solid pastoral network. They loved their church and served in many capacities.

"It happened slowly, over time," Tim started. "Jeffrey, our minister, is a pastoral man. He has a love in his heart bigger than Chicago itself. After eighteen years as St. Jude's pastor, the people trusted him, loved him, and followed his leadership faithfully. But that gift of compassion is what got him in trouble."

"It became more important than the truth of God's Word," Sandy interjected.

"See," Tim continued, "Jeffrey believes the heart of the gospel message is the love of God. Christians are to experience that love, share His love with each other, and evangelize the world by loving as Christ loves us. Now, that's hard to argue with. Plus, that's Jeffrey. It is who he is, what he preaches, and the thrust of the ministry at St. Jude's.

"For example, we have an incredible social outreach to the poor in our community. We sponsor a halfway home for prisoners, a soup kitchen, a shelter for the homeless, and a used clothing operation that has citywide recognition. We are a church that does more than talk about love."

"So when did you know something was wrong?" I asked.

"Like Tim said," Sandy said with a certain confidence, "it happened slowly. But one day we realized that the church had not baptized anyone for a long time. So, one Sunday morning, after services, we were having coffee and Jeffrey came over. In the course of the discussion, we asked him why it had been so long since someone was baptized.

"We couldn't believe his answer. He said, 'We don't do that any more. A year-and-a-half ago, the board of elders adopted a new policy to discontinue baptisms at St. Jude's. Baptism assumes that there are people inside God's kingdom and people outside his kingdom. This goes against every aspect of God's love for his children. We are to love everybody and not put up any barriers! So instead of baptizing, we welcome anyone and everyone who comes.'"

"That was the first time," Tim came in, "that we realized St. Jude's had embraced the doctrine of universal salvation. This means they believed everyone is saved regardless of whether or not a person confesses Jesus Christ and His death on the cross for their lives. We pursued the matter with the church elders. This was exactly their stand. But that's just the beginning. It gets worse."

"What do you mean?" I inquired.

"Well, for example, the board of elders agreed that Jeffrey did not have to stick with the biblical view of marriage. They gave him permission to bless couples who are living together outside the covenant of marriage. This includes same-sex unions. It's all part of Jeffrey's loving and accepting everyone just as they are. And the elders were in complete agreement at every step."

"Once we knew," Tim went on, "we could not sit back and watch. We first met with Jeffrey. We outlined from the Scriptures the traditional view of salvation in Jesus Christ, the purpose for baptism, God's love for the sinner and yet his wrath against sin, and then the view of holy matrimony. We were loving and careful. But he utterly rejected us. He could not hear."

"We did not stop there," Sandy continued. "We met with the board of elders and made the same presentation. They too rejected us. They called us fundamentalists, Bible thumpers, unloving and prejudiced snobs. One of them asked us to leave the church. Another told us that we were divisive and threatened us if we tried to start a faction at St. Jude's."

"At an open forum in the church," Tim said, "Sandy and I stood up and announced our leaving. In those few moments, we spoke out against the doctrines Jeffrey and the board had adopted in recent years. When we finished speaking, Jeffrey told the congregation that they needed to pray for us, for we were deceived by the fundamentalists. There was not a hint of anger in Jeffrey's voice. No, he said it with deep compassion, as though he truly loved us. And, before we could respond to the charge, he closed the meeting."

Tim and Sandy were deceivers in the sight of the church.

They went to the pastor. He could not listen. They went to the elders. They were united as one people against the Zimmermans' prophetic voice. Lastly, Tim and Sandy went to the church. In this case, the church had lost the ability to hear.

Like Martin Luther of old, who held high the standard of sound biblical doctrine, Tim and Sandy confronted the deceiver in their day. And they were too late—the Eden serpent had already won an entire church.

From Individual to Corporate Deception

Corporate deception happens one of two ways. The first begins when a small group of people—caught in deception and unable to hear the church's testimony—leave the church and set out on their own. Often they are driven by discouragement and the longing to prove they are right and blessed of God.

They find others to join them. Perhaps they meet regularly. Maybe they grow in size. Slowly, a new church community is built, one birthed in deception and the ongoing practice of not hearing. Paul wrote about this, the emergence of a deceived community:

> For the time will come when they will not endure
> sound doctrine; but wanting to have their ears
> tickled, they will accumulate for themselves teachers
> in accordance to their own desires; and will turn

away their ears from the truth, and will turn aside to myths (2 Tim. 4:3-4).

A man-made, deceptive Christianity begins when the deceived turn their ears from the truth. The listening process stops. Not being able to endure sound doctrine, they "accumulate ... teachers in accordance to their own desires." And a new church is founded.

There's a second way corporate deception evolves. It starts slowly. Rituals without meaning set in, traditions done over and over. Even the most Christ-centered activity can switch into meaningless repetition if He isn't the living, present Lord of the activity.

For example, Jesus Himself stood against the Ephesians: "But I have this against you, that you have left your first love" (Rev. 2:4). Gradually, a church done *for* Jesus—not *with* Jesus— forms. If it continues on that track, in routine, without repentance, then the church will fall into deception and lose its ability to hear:

> Because you say, "I am rich, and have become wealthy, and have need of nothing," and you do not know that you are wretched and miserable and poor and blind and naked ... behold, I [Jesus] stand at the door and knock (Rev. 3:17, 20a).

This church in Laodicea models a non-hearing church. They believed they were rich, wealthy and in need of nothing. The Lord Jesus Christ told them differently. But they could not hear His voice. He was standing outside their door, knocking.

Corporate deception: It's the gathering of a Christian body that cannot hear the Savior's voice—but it thinks it can. It's the sign marking the end times and is the subject of the final chapter.

The Commitment to Prayer

When the door opens and the deceived leave the church, what does the Christian community do? We pray unceasingly.

We intercede for their protection. We pray for the Lord to break through the blindness to see His light, through the deafness to hear His voice.

The simple, wooden chapel swelled with sounds of praise and thanksgiving. The midsummer sun shone through the lofty stained-glass windows down upon the altar set with bread and wine. It was Sunday morning. Erilynne and I were concluding a weekend retreat in Warwick, New York, with people offering their testimonies.

"I give thanks to the Lord Jesus for my son!" Phyllis said. "It was three years ago today that Ricky came home. All that time in the drug underworld, and still the Lord brought him back to me."

"Oh, God—my son! My son!" a sobbing cry went out.

Over in the front corner pew, a couple had fallen into each other's arms crying with loud wails. It was Jess and Kelly Scott. As we brought them up, a number of people from the congregation moved forward.

"We're sorry, Phyllis," Jess said. "But our son has not come home. It has been four years. He left without ever speaking to us again. No letters. No phone calls—nothing. We've tried to see him, but he ignores us. He acts like we're not even there. His eyes—so cold, so hard."

"We've lost our son," Kelly wept.

"I know their son Richard," a man said behind Kelly. "Before he left the church, he was in my Bible study class. I know he met the Lord. I was there the day he received Jesus Christ into his heart."

"It's that church," someone said in the back.

"It all started when Richard fell in love with this college woman," the man continued. "She happened to go to this church, invited Richard, and we have never seen him since. He and the young woman broke up a long time ago—but Richard stayed. The minister took him under his wing. It's supposed to be a Christian church, but it's not. It's a cult."

"Everything they do is in Christ's name," Jess said. "We're told Richard lives with Christians who hear God's will for him. He's told what he can and cannot do."

Kelly looked up at me, her eyes swollen red, "I don't care. I just want him back. After four years, how long can I wait?"

"We've prayed every day for him," Jess said. "These brothers and sisters have walked through it with us. We couldn't have made it without their prayers and encouragement. We know Richard belongs to Jesus, and we believe He's going to bring our son home again—safe."

We circled around Jess and Kelly. As we began to pray, Kelly started to sob bitterly again, then Jess, then all of us. "Open Richard's ears to hear, Holy Spirit," we prayed. "Open his eyes to see. Open his heart to know only Your truth. Bless him today."

The passion for praying comes from the soul that longs for a person to see Jesus Christ. There are people to this very day that Erilynne and I pray unceasingly for—who remain blinded from the light of Christ. Sometimes prayers are not answered. The person's will remains set, immovable. But still we pray, interceding for the person's heart to turn to the waiting arms of the Lord. And when it happens, there is rejoicing in heaven and earth!

Six weeks after the Warwick retreat, on a hot August afternoon, the phone rang. It was a Catholic priest from a neighboring town. "Your son, Richard, has spent the day with me. He came here because he is scared. He doesn't know where to go. He has left his church against its wishes, and he's not sure you want him home. I thought I'd call."

Richard was home that very afternoon—at last.

It took months to walk through the pain of four years of separation and the cultic views held by the church. But Richard began to heal. The more time went by, the more Richard could see the power of deception.

"They looked so Christian," he said a few weeks later. "I really thought those people spoke for God. I just couldn't see it. One day, it was like I woke up and came to my senses. It was wrong to have left my family. It was wrong to put all my trust in this minister and what he wanted me to do. That's when I knew—I had to get out of there."

Unceasing prayer. When believers are stuck in deafening deception, when they leave the church community, our commitment to them doesn't end. No matter what the issue is, no matter how difficult the problem, we must remain in constant prayer for them in the hope that one day they might have ears to hear—and be won.

Twenty-One

THE LAST DAYS

"Go, and tell this people: 'Keep on listening, but do not perceive; keep on looking, but do not understand.' Render the hearts of this people insensitive, their ears dull, and their eyes dim, lest they see with their eyes, hear with their ears, understand with their hearts, and return and be healed" (Isa. 6:9-10).

Isaiah was not sent to uncircumcised pagans. He was sent to his own people: the nation of Israel. He was God's mouthpiece to a generation of Jews who sincerely believed they walked with God. His orders: to proclaim the word of the Lord. His problem: Israel could no longer hear. Deception had fallen on an entire people.

How is that possible? We know from Isaiah that the Jewish leadership had exchanged the present, living relationship with the Lord God for a cheap replica. That replica was nothing less than a counterfeit, man-made religion.

It happens every time the faithful stop listening. For when the hearing stops, the vital, dynamic relationship with the Lord stops. In its place, patterns of religious activity form: outward ceremonies, full of rituals and traditions, performed without meaning, without the inward conversion of the heart.

God's people do God-things. In Isaiah's day, they kept His commandments, offered sacrifices, attended services, honored the appointed feasts, recited endless prayers, and studied His Word. They performed the right God things. But where was the relationship? It was gone, lost like a marriage full of activity but without love.

Isaiah rightly prophesied God's word: "Because this people draw near with their words and honor Me with their lip service, but they remove their hearts far from Me, and their reverence for Me consists of tradition learned by rote ..." (Isa. 29:13).

Deception permeated the entire nation of Israel. The Jewish leaders stopped hearing and speaking God's living word. They became masters of ceremonies, caretakers in the religious museum of God's historic activity. In His name, they erected traditions that allowed Israel to worship their Lord—without ever hearing His present voice in their generation. Their hearts were far from Him. The personal relationship with the Lord, bearing the kind of intimacy revealed by the writers of the psalms, mattered no more.

It's the pattern that Scripture teaches of corporate deception.

First, the leadership and the people stop hearing God. Second, in place of the daily, personal relationship with Him, religious activities form, rituals without meaning, performed by rote. Third, a powerless God-looking but man-made religion emerges. Its leaders cannot hear the Lord, but they know how to make a not-listening religion flourish in His name.

It's corporate deception, for this godlike religion becomes the accepted norm in society—the "right" way to find God. The people sincerely believe their religion is holy and true, but they are deceived. They can't hear Him. They continue to perform their godly rituals fully expecting that when they die they will go to heaven. They have no clue that their path leads straight into Satan's fire.

And God sends His messengers, His prophets—even His Son. He lifts up His voice to His people. He calls out, but He is not heard. Deception has made their ears dull, their eyes dim, and their hearts insensitive. But it does not stop there. Traditionally, the deaf elders of the faith turn against God's messengers. In the name of the Lord, they silence the prophets that are sent to them. Some they persecute. Others they kill. This always happens when deception has run its full course. The voice of God's servants has to be stopped—snuffed out like a candle at midnight.

Jesus

Jesus of Nazareth was anointed by God "with the Holy Spirit and with power" (Acts 10:38). He spoke the fresh, living word of the Lord for all to hear. He performed the miraculous for all to see. This was the beloved Son of God—the eternal second Person of the Trinity—Jesus, conceived by the Holy Spirit and born of a woman. God had become real, true man, just as the prophets said.

It was the "fulness of time" (Gal. 4:4). He, their promised Messiah and long-awaited Savior, "came to His own, and those who were His own did not receive Him" (John 1:11). It was the day of their "visitation" (Luke 19:44), but they didn't have ears to hear.

Once more, as it was in Isaiah's day, deception had come to an entire people. The shift had happened. Their present relationship with the Lord God Almighty, their covenant God, had vanished, and in its stead, dressed in disguise, stood a counterfeit—a godlike religion, all too real in appearance. The people of Israel had tossed aside the living God, and they didn't know it.

The Isaiah prophecy was back. Jesus lifted His voice, quoting the exact prophecy of Isaiah 6:

"You will keep on hearing, but will not understand;

and you will keep on seeing, but will not perceive; for the heart of this people has become dull, and with their ears they scarcely hear, and they have closed their eyes lest they should see with their eyes, and hear with their ears, and understand with their heart and return, and I should heal them" (Matt. 13:14-15).

Like Isaiah, Jesus lived in a day when deception was rampant.

His generation could not hear. It started with the leaders: "Why do you not understand what I am saying?" Jesus asked them. "It is because you cannot hear My word" (John 8:43). He said the same thing to His soon-to-be murderers:

Woe to you, scribes and Pharisees, hypocrites! For you build the tombs of the prophets and adorn the monuments of the righteous, and say, "If we had been living in the days of our fathers, we would not have been partners with them in shedding the blood of the prophets" (Matt. 23:29-31).

The Lord Jesus caught them in their wicked, deafening deception. He watched them build up the tombs of the dead prophets. He heard them say with assurance, "We wouldn't have killed the prophets! Not like our fathers." And He knew that they were no different than their fathers. Their boasting, their pride, was hypocrisy. For these same people, thinking they were different, were not. Soon they would nail Jesus of Nazareth, the Son of the living God, to the cross.

There are two major principles about deception that arise from this story. First, we must notice that the leaders could hear the dead prophets but not the living prophets. Why? Because godlike religion can only hear God's Word from history. What it can't hear is God speaking in the present day.

In other words, it is safe to hear what the Lord demanded from other generations. It is safe to stay at a distance, study the history, even memorize the words. But when those words come alive in the here and now, when the biblical commands are no longer historical, but are God speaking to us today, calling us to hear, change, and follow Him, then it is no longer safe.

In every generation, the Lord promises to speak His Word. The canon of Scripture is closed. But He is still making His Word alive, gently beckoning all who can hear to enter into a personal, saving relationship with Him. Without it, all that is left is a man-made, look-alike religion that does not know Him and cannot hear His voice. As a result, these Jewish leaders who honored the dead prophets were altogether deaf. They could not hear the Son of God as He spoke right in front of them. This phenomenon of hearing the dead but not the living is a primary mark of deception.

So Jesus continually said, "He who has ears to hear, let him hear" (Luke 14:35). The Word must be "living and active," piercing our souls in the present and causing us to live fully and only for Christ.

There is a second principle. It is more difficult to understand. As the Jewish leaders adorned the monuments of the righteous, they testified that these servants had been unjustly murdered. Their fathers had heard the prophets speak but did not believe these men were sent by God—so the fathers killed them. They stamped out their voices, coldly and silently, fully convinced their voice came from hell, not heaven. And they did it believing they were rendering a pleasing service to the Lord (see John 16:2).

Stephen's last words before he died spoke directly to the principle:

> You men who are stiff-necked and uncircumcised in heart and ears are always resisting the Holy Spirit; you are doing just as your fathers did. Which one of the prophets did your fathers not persecute? And they killed those who had previously announced the coming of the Righteous One, whose betrayers and murderers you have now become (Acts 7: 51-52).

He called the Jewish leaders uncircumcised in heart and

ears. The sins of the fathers had been passed down. As their fathers could not hear the preaching of God's Word in their day, so neither could the children. And the response is violent: The fathers persecuted and killed the prophets who foretold the coming of Jesus. The children did worse: They betrayed and then murdered the Savior when He came. The cycle of stamping out God's living Word repeats itself over and over.

It did not stop with the Savior.

Stephen finished his last words and was killed. His death in the New Testament is a living promise that the Christian era would resound with the same principle. Those who proclaim God's Word are silenced. They are hard to hear. And, in the last days, when deception increases even more, these servants will be silenced, sent away, even snuffed out—and that by the religious leaders of the day.

The Holy Spirit

Jesus said: "I will ask the Father, and He will give you another Helper, that He may be with you forever" (John 14:16). That was the plan. The Lord would ascend to His throne of glory. Yet, He would not leave us as "orphans" (John 14:18). Father would send God the Holy Spirit to the church. And He did—on Pentecost morning.

That plan has not changed:

> But when He, the Spirit of truth, comes, He will guide you into all the truth; for He will not speak on His own initiative, but whatever He hears, He will speak; and He will disclose to you what is to come (John 16:13).

The Spirit of the living God is a listener. His ministry on earth begins with hearing. This is the promise: "Whatever He hears, He will speak." By so doing, He guides the church into all truth.

The Holy Spirit of truth is here today. He speaks in the

present and calls believers personally and the church corporately into that living relationship with our Lord Jesus Christ. But here's the most important question of all: Are we truly listening to what the Holy Spirit is saying *today?*

Do we have ears to hear?

Even though the Holy Spirit came to the church at Pentecost, the deceiver's work goes on. The Eden serpent now centers his mission on the church. He seeks to block the ears of Christians, to cut off our fellowship with the Holy Spirit, and to turn our living relationship with the Lord Jesus Christ into a dead, meaningless tradition done by rote. His greatest desire is to bring about corporate deception, as in Isaiah's day and the Savior's day. Satan's ultimate goal is to sever the church from the living voice of the Holy Spirit speaking God's Word in our day—to make dead Christianity flourish.

On that day, the church will have no witness in the world, no gospel to proclaim, and therefore no one radically converted from darkness to light, from the dominion of Satan to God, from death to eternal life in Christ Jesus (see Acts 26:18).

Why can't we learn this truth from Scripture? Are the warnings not clear enough? Yet, even in the New Testament, we witness the serpent back at work. Why couldn't the Christians stop him? They saw him capture their own Lord and Savior—dressed in the garments of the Jewish leaders. These same men professed to have the blood of Abraham in their bodies and the Law of Moses in their hearts.

So why didn't the Christians know? The Eden serpent always works to turn God's people away from a living relationship with Him. He always works to create a deadly, look-alike counterfeit, a godlike religion that cannot hear Him—one that drowns out His voice each time He speaks.

They did know! So why couldn't the New Testament Christian leaders stop the deceiver from working in the community of faith?

How quickly the church fell to deception. For example, five of the seven churches in Revelation (chapters two and three) had allowed the deceiver in. We see the serpent in Ephesus steal their hearts from their first love, Jesus Christ. The last church, Laodicea, had permitted the deceiver to work so effectively that the Lord Jesus was not even in the church. He was outside. The deceiver had made the Laodiceans deaf. So the Savior said, "Behold, I stand at the door and knock; if anyone hears My voice" ... (Rev. 3:20).

To each of the seven churches, the risen Lord spoke the same message: *"He who has an ear, let him hear what the Spirit says to the churches"* (Rev. 2:7, italics added).

The Lord Jesus Christ made it so clear. He asked His Father, and the Father sent God the Holy Spirit to the church, alive and present, here and now. With confidence today, we can receive the Holy Spirit into our hearts and into our churches. We can know the Spirit of truth who is given to speak whatever He hears, to guide us into all truth, to keep us, His very own, in daily communion with the Lord Jesus Christ. His presence with us in the church community is the one and only way to protect believers from the work of the deceiver of old.

We must stay together as Christians. We have got to have ears to hear what the Holy Spirit is saying to the churches in our generation. Do you have ears to hear?

Remember Eve

Hearing. Nothing matters half so much.

"But I am afraid," Paul wrote, "lest as the serpent deceived Eve by his craftiness, your minds should be led astray from the simplicity and purity of devotion to Christ. For if one comes and preaches another Jesus ..." (2 Cor. 11:3-4).

There's another Jesus. He is a deceiver.

He came in the glory of Eden. His garment of light appeared radiant, dazzling white, like any other serpent God had made.

His disguise, so convincing, gave him authority to speak God's Word.

And Eve listened. She had no reason to disbelieve the serpent. As she went to the tree, only one thing was required of her.

She needed right then and there to turn to her God-given relationships. Eve lived in covenant community with the Lord her God and Adam her husband. Had she gathered them together before eating, had she consulted them about the serpent's words, the deception would have failed—instantly! The mask would have melted away in the presence of God Almighty. And there Satan would have stood—naked in the glory of God, exposed for all to see.

But she didn't call on that relationship.

It's for this reason that Paul told us to remember Eve. The same could happen to you and me and to our church. For many deceivers have appeared in the church today. Their job is to exchange our relationship to Jesus Christ and His community for an outward, godlike religion. They want us to believe the Holy Spirit isn't speaking clearly in our day.

But we must not heed them. It is our duty, at all times and in every way, to call on our God-given relationships.

If we don't, deception will flourish in the church. And this will most certainly take place, for the Scriptures teach that corporate deception will happen again in the last days. "And many false prophets will arise, and will mislead many" (Matt. 24:11). It will come with "all power and signs and false wonders, and with all the deception of wickedness" (2 Thess. 2:9-10). "But evil men and impostors will proceed from bad to worse, deceiving and being deceived" (2 Tim. 3:13).

Just as it was in Jesus' day, godlike religion will be the accepted norm. And the Holy Spirit will raise up messengers to preach the Word of God to that generation. These servants will lift their voice to the churches, but they will not be heard. Once again, like the pattern of old, these servants will be silenced, their voices hushed, their lives persecuted, and they will be killed.

And the Isaiah 6 passage will be fulfilled in that day too:

> Go and tell this people: 'Keep on listening, but do not perceive; keep on looking, but do not understand.' Render the hearts of this people insensitive, their ears dull, and their eyes dim, lest they see with their eyes, hear with their ears, understand with their hearts, and return and be healed (Isa. 6:9-10).

This exhortation begs God's people to enter fully into the covenant relationship we have been given in the Lord. If we return, we will be healed. That promise is true today. Every time we turn to the Lord Jesus and His people, He will open our ears to hear, our eyes to see, and our hearts to understand. He will take away the power of deception in our lives—but we must turn to Him. We must find a people who belong to Him, who are saved by the blood of the Lamb, who hold to the testimony of the redeeming power of the Lord Jesus Christ.

In those last days, we must pray to have ears that hear.

We write these things so that you may not be deceived. Be on guard for yourselves and for all the flock. Be on the alert! Stay in relationship to the Lord Jesus. Call on His name. Do not walk alone but remain together in fellowship with those who belong to Jesus. Devote yourselves to praying daily in the Holy Spirit. If you have ears to hear, hear what the Spirit says to the churches.

And no matter what, remember Eve.